Emotion: A Very Short Introduction

Praise for the first edition

'a pop science classic'

Walsh, *Independent on Sunday*

'At last, an accessible and fascinating account of a neglected aspect of our mental lives.'

Lewis Wolpert, author of *Malignant Sadness*

'Anyone who wants a brief introduction to what is going on in thinking and research on emotions could not do better than this book by Dylan Evans. It connects with important issues of our time, including the origins of emotions, how far they can be controlled, and why they are important to us—a lively and lovely book.'

Keith Oatley, University of Toronto

'The science of emotions for the Ecstasy generation—with warmth and good humor, Evans argues persuasively that the human heart embodies a socially attuned wisdom that is deeper, broader, and more adaptive than conscious rationality. The best short introduction to the human passions.'

Geoffrey Miller, author of *The Mating Mind*

'Dylan Evans, one of the best of the new wave of science writers, has written a masterly survey—lean, confident, and packed with up-to-the-minute information. It will enlighten and surprise.'

Nicholas Humphrey, author of *A History of the Mind*
and *Leaps of Faith*

VERY SHORT INTRODUCTIONS are for anyone wanting a stimulating and accessible way into a new subject. They are written by experts, and have been translated into more than 45 different languages.

The series began in 1995, and now covers a wide variety of topics in every discipline. The VSI library currently contains over 600 volumes—a Very Short Introduction to everything from Psychology and Philosophy of Science to American History and Relativity—and continues to grow in every subject area.

Very Short Introductions available now:

Available soon:

For more information visit our website

www.oup.com/vsi/

Dylan Evans

EMOTION

A Very Short Introduction

SECOND EDITION

OXFORD
UNIVERSITY PRESS

OXFORD
UNIVERSITY PRESS

Great Clarendon Street, Oxford, OX2 6DP,
United Kingdom

Oxford University Press is a department of the University of Oxford.
It furthers the University's objective of excellence in research, scholarship,
and education by publishing worldwide. Oxford is a registered trade mark of
Oxford University Press in the UK and in certain other countries

First published 2001
First published as a Very Short Introduction 2003
Second edition published 2019

Published in the United States of America by Oxford University Press
198 Madison Avenue, New York, NY 10016, United States of America

British Library Cataloguing in Publication Data
Data available

Library of Congress Control Number: 2019941402

ISBN 978-0-19-883440-3

Printed and bound by CPI Group (UK) Ltd, Croydon, CR0 4YY

Contents

Preface to the second edition

This is a fully revised and updated edition of *Emotion: A Very Short Introduction*, which was first published under the title *Emotion: The Science of Sentiment* in 2001. A great deal has happened in research on emotions since then, and this new edition incorporates some of these new developments. However, the main outlines of the story remain the same.

The scientific study of emotion owes much to the philosophers of the Enlightenment. David Hume, Adam Smith, and Thomas Reid all wrote at length about the sentiments and the passions. These thinkers believed that emotions were vital to individual and social existence. Smith did not just found the 'dismal science' (economics); he also helped to pioneer the 'sentimental science' (the psychology of emotion). In his first book, *The Theory of Moral Sentiments* (1759), he proposed that emotions were the thread that wove together the fabric of society. Like Hume and Reid, Smith did not regard emotion and thought as implacable enemies. For all of these thinkers, it was rational to be emotional, and no science of the mind could be complete without also addressing the heart.

The Romantics rejected this view, reviving an older view of emotions as fundamentally at odds with reason. Humans were faced with a stark choice between emotion and reason, and the wise ones chose to follow their hearts rather than their heads. To return to innocence meant listening to one's feelings rather than consulting logic. The secrets of sentiment were to be unlocked by poetry, not by science.

I have a great deal of sympathy with the Enlightenment view of emotion. Unlike the Romantics, I do not believe that emotions are fundamentally at odds with reason, nor that we should always follow our hearts rather than our heads. Rather, like Adam Smith, I believe that intelligent action results from a harmonious blend of emotion and reason. I believe that a creature without emotions would be less rational than us, not more, but I also believe that there are times when it is better to listen to the head rather than the heart. Knowing when to follow our feelings and when to ignore them is a valuable talent that some have called 'emotional intelligence'.

In this book I argue for a return to the view of emotions as reason's ally, not its enemy. Like Smith and Hume, I believe that the scientific study of emotion is not only possible, but of great value. This is not because I think we can ever reduce emotional experience to a dry formula. However, thinking more clearly about emotion need not be opposed to feeling more deeply. It is my hope that knowing more about how emotions work can help us to lead richer lives, not poorer. At the very least, it can be exciting to learn about the recent scientific advances in our understanding of these mysterious phenomena.

Scientific interest in the emotions underwent something of a renaissance in the 1990s. For much of the 20th century, research in the emotions was confined to a few psychologists and even fewer anthropologists. Today, however, things are rather different. Emotion is now a hot topic. Many anthropologists now reject the view that emotions are culturally specific. Cognitive psychologists have abandoned their exclusive focus on reasoning, perception, and memory, and are rediscovering the importance of affective processes. Neuroscientists and researchers in artificial intelligence have also joined the debate, contributing further pieces to the jigsaw. This book attempts to step back and put some of these pieces together.

Needless to say, a short book like this cannot hope to cover all aspects of such a complex area. I have had to leave some very interesting areas of emotion research to one side. The reader will not find, for example, a discussion of how emotions develop in children, although this too is a burgeoning area of study. Nor is there any mention of the growing literature on individual differences in emotional experience. My choice of topics reflects my own idiosyncratic interests and my guesses about what will prove most interesting to a general audience.

The word 'emotion' is fairly recent. Before the 19th century, people talked instead about 'passions', 'sentiments', and 'affections'. Chapter 1 begins by outlining the complex history of these words. It then goes on to explore the variety of emotional experience in different cultures. Every culture has its own emotional climate, and I draw on anthropological research that has documented some of these variations. However, many anthropologists now think that the differences between emotional experiences around the world are minor when compared with the similarities. In Chapter 1 I argue that emotions constitute a kind of 'universal language' that binds humanity together into a single family. Our common emotional heritage goes deeper than the cultural differences that set us apart.

We owe this shared emotional repertoire to our common ancestry. We are all descended from a few thousand hominids who lived on the African plains 100,000 years ago. Many of our emotions were forged in this bygone age. Many more emotions go back even further, to a time when our ancestors were not even human. In Chapter 2 I explore the evolutionary history of emotion and argue that emotions were—and still are—vital for survival. Emotions are not just luxuries. Still less are they obstacles to intelligent action, as many philosophers have believed. The creators of *Star Trek* were wrong to suppose that the Vulcans, an imaginary alien race that had learned to suppress their emotions, would be more intelligent than humans. Spock notwithstanding, an intelligent creature that lacked emotions simply could not evolve.

Of course, we now live in very different environments from those in which our ancestors evolved. In particular, we have many means of inducing happiness in ourselves that our ancestors never even dreamt of. In Chapter 3 I discuss these 'technologies of mood' that promise to provide us with short cuts to happiness, from psychotherapy and art to drugs and meditation. I ask whether or not they work and discuss the dangers that beset some of these attempts to circumvent the more circuitous path to happiness that natural selection laid out for us.

In Chapter 4 I explain how emotions affect 'cognitive' capacities such as memory, attention, and perception. The power of emotions to affect these things makes emotional technologies very appealing to advertisers and politicians. Appealing to feelings offers a way of making people change their minds without having to provide good arguments or evidence. I conclude the chapter by exploring some of the recent research in the psychology and neuroscience of empathy.

The most recent discipline to have entered the debate on emotion is artificial intelligence. Since the early 1990s, computer scientists have become increasingly interested in building emotional machines, and workers in robotics are already making some progress in this area. In the final chapter I discuss these recent developments and speculate on where it will all lead. Will we succeed in building robots that have feelings just like we do? And what might be the consequences of such technology? Research in this area is moving fast, and I have completely rewritten this chapter to reflect the advances that have taken place since the first edition of this book was published in 2001.

I do not pretend to have the last word on emotion. A really good theory of emotion may remain forever beyond our grasp. However, I find the scientific study of emotion illuminating and fascinating. I hope that reading this book will lead you to share my enthusiasm.

Dylan Evans

October 2018

List of illustrations

Emotion

Chapter 1
What is an emotion?

The word *emotion* is a modern invention—and not a particularly
helpful one. The first books to use the word in the title do not
appear until the 19th century. The most famous of these is
The Expression of the Emotions in Man and Animals, by Charles
Darwin, which was published in 1872.

Philosophers and poets had been writing about things like anger,
pity, and fear for thousands of years, of course, but they had never
before grouped these mental states together under a single
umbrella. On the contrary, they had been more concerned to draw
distinctions between them, categorizing some of them as passions
and desires, and others as affections and sentiments. Thus, when
the Scottish psychologist Alexander Bain announced, in his 1859
book *The Emotions and the Will*, that he would use the word
emotion to cover to 'all that is understood by feelings, states of
feeling, pleasures, pains, passions, sentiments, affections', he was
marking a fundamental shift in the vocabulary that we use to
describe how the mind works.

Behind this terminological shift lay a deeper conceptual
revolution—the birth of modern psychology, a self-professed
'scientific' approach to the study of the mind, modelled on the
natural sciences, especially physiology. The pioneers of this new

approach were explicit about their desire to break with traditional ways of discussing and studying the mind, which were inextricably bound up with theology and ethics.

Take theology first. The emergence of scientific psychology in the 19th century was closely linked with the decline of Christianity among the elites in Europe and North America. Scientific psychology was explicitly cast as a new, thoroughly secular approach to the study of the mind, in contrast to the long tradition of Christian thought which had dominated this and most other areas of study in the West for the previous fifteen centuries. Words like *passion*, *lust*, and *desire* all had a biblical pedigree which the pioneers of scientific psychology wished to dispense with. The term *passion* in particular was associated with the Gospel accounts of the sufferings and death of Jesus. By replacing all these words with a term like *emotion*, which was free of such connotations, the new scientific approach signalled its distance from theological ways of thinking.

Even older than the theological framework was that of ethics. Long before Christianity had appeared on the scene, the philosophers of Ancient Greece had given a central place to things like pity, fear, and anger in their debates about the good life. Plato (c.428–348 BC) famously divided the mind into three distinct faculties or elements: reason, appetite, and *thumos*, which can be variously translated as 'anger', 'spirit', or 'indignation'. This analysis seems distinctly odd from a modern perspective. Contemporary psychologists might wonder why Plato singles out anger from the other emotions and reserves a whole faculty of the mind for this particular feeling. What about sadness, fear, and guilt? Where do they figure in this account? Yet this simply highlights the distance between ancient approaches to the mind and that of today. Psychologists may now group together a variety of mental states in a single category called emotions, but that is a modern invention, and would have made no sense in Ancient Greece.

For Plato, the whole point of dividing the mind into three distinct parts was to understand how best to live. It was not what we today would call a 'scientific' exercise, which is supposed to be objective and value-neutral, but an ethical one. The good person, in Plato's view, is one in whom all three elements of the mind are in harmony, and each element performs its proper function. This is only possible, Plato taught, when both appetite and *thumos* are subordinated to reason.

This idea was developed into a whole system of thought by another Greek philosopher, Zeno of Citium (*c.*334–262 BC), the founder of Stoicism. The Stoics taught that the good life consisted in freedom from all passions (*pathê*). The passions, as the Stoics understood the term, were strong feelings that troubled the mind such as intense anger and excessive joy. The passions, they argued, are like mistaken opinions, since they arise from putting too much value on things that are not really so important. The wise person does not value trivial things, and so attains peace of mind (*apatheia*). This is not a complete absence of feeling; on the contrary, the Stoic who judges things correctly experiences contentment (*eudaimonia*) and good feelings (*eupatheiai*), but these are mild and sweet rather than strong and stormy.

Stoicism has been a remarkably persistent influence in Western thought. Far from dying out with the rise of Christianity, it was woven into theology by Christian thinkers from Boethius (477–524) to Justus Lipsius (1547–1606). But there is something odd about this, as there is about many other attempts to combine Christianity with Greek philosophy. The founder of Christianity is quite the opposite of a serene Stoic. Jesus flies into a holy rage when he sees the temple in Jerusalem filled with merchants and money changers, and drives them out of the temple with a whip. When he is dying on the cross, he cries out in agony: 'My God, my God, why have you forsaken me?' A major strand of Christian piety celebrates these strong emotions, from Saint Augustine to

Saint John of the Cross. As Martha Nussbaum observes, the Christian idea of love is unashamedly passionate, even erotic:

> We hear sighs of longing and groans of profound desolation. We hear love songs composed in anguish, as the singer's heart strains upward in desire. We hear of a hunger that cannot be satisfied, of a thirst that torments, of the taste of a lover's body that kindles inexpressible longing. We hear of an opening that longs for penetration, of a burning fire that ignites the body and the heart. All these are images of a profound erotic passion. And all of these are images of Christian love.

Whatever the relationship between Stoicism and Christianity may be, the self-professed 'scientific' approach to the mind that arose in the 19th century wanted to dispense with both of these traditions. Psychology was to be morally neutral, free from the ethical framework in which the Greek philosophers had couched their approach to the mind, and completely secular, free of religious connotations. And to make this abundantly clear, psychologists needed a new vocabulary. The word *emotion* fitted this need perfectly.

The problem was, nobody knew what the new word really meant. When the Edinburgh professor of moral philosophy, Thomas Brown, used the term in his lectures in 1810–20, he told his students that 'the exact meaning of the term *emotion* is difficult to state in any form of words'. Two centuries later, things are not much clearer. Psychologists still disagree about how to define the term. As the philosopher Thomas Dixon wryly observes, 'this is hardly surprising for a term that, from the outset, was defined as being indefinable'.

Yet this may not be as much of a problem as it seems. For although a precise definition may prove elusive, it remains true, as Thomas Brown stated in his Edinburgh lectures 200 years ago, that 'every person understands what is meant by an emotion'. The word emotion may, in other words, be rather like jazz, in the sense that you know it when you see it, or feel it, even though you can't define it. Or, as the jazz musician Louis Armstrong famously quipped, 'If you have to ask what jazz is, you'll never know.'

Basic emotions

Instead of attempting to provide a concise definition of emotion, it may be more fruitful to identify some typical examples. Few people would deny that anger, fear, and joy are emotions. When it comes to enumerating a complete list of emotions, however, there is little consensus. The British psychologist Simon Baron-Cohen identified close to 1,000 emotion words in the adult English lexicon and classified them into 23 mutually exclusive categories. Other researchers argue for a smaller number of categories.

In an attempt to make sense of these widely differing approaches, the philosopher Paul Griffiths divides emotions into three distinct groups: basic emotions, higher cognitive emotions, and culturally specific emotions. Basic emotions include joy, distress, anger, fear, surprise, and disgust (see Box 1). Basic emotions are universal and innate. This much is clear from the fact that babies who are born blind still make the facial expressions typical of these emotions—smiling, grimacing, and so on. Emotional expressions are not like words, which differ from culture to culture; they are closer to breathing, which is just part of human nature.

For a large part of the 20th century, many anthropologists rejected the idea that any emotions were universal or innate, for they subscribed to a view known as the cultural theory of emotion. According to this view, emotions are learned behaviours, transmitted culturally, much like languages. Just as you must first hear English before you can speak it, so you must first see others being joyful before you can feel joy. On this theory, people living in different cultures should experience different emotions.

Box 1 Basic emotions

Basic emotions are universal and innate. They are of rapid onset and last a few seconds at a time. Researchers disagree about how many basic emotions there are, but most would include the following in their list:

- Joy
- Distress
- Anger
- Fear
- Surprise
- Disgust

Some researchers call these emotions by different names. It is common, for example, to see 'happiness' and 'sadness' in the list of basic emotions. I think these words are better used to describe moods rather than emotions (see Chapter 3), so in this book I use the words 'joy' and 'distress' to refer to basic emotions and reserve the terms 'happiness' and 'sadness' for good and bad moods.

In the late 1960s, while this view of emotion was still the reigning orthodoxy, a young American anthropologist called Paul Ekman set out to find firm scientific evidence in its favour. To his great surprise, he ended up doing just the opposite. Ekman's studies provided the first scientific evidence that the cultural theory of emotion was badly off the mark.

Ekman's methodology was simple but clever. He travelled to a remote, preliterate culture (the Fore, in New Guinea) to ensure that the subjects had not seen Western photographs or films, and so could never have learned Western emotions. Ekman then told them various stories, and asked them to choose, from three photographs of Americans expressing various emotions, the photo that most closely matched the story.

For example, one story involved coming across a wild pig when alone in a hut, a situation that would elicit fear in Westerners. Sure enough, the Fore pointed to the same expressions that Westerners linked to the stories. Just to be sure, Ekman asked some Fore people to make facial expressions appropriate to each of the stories and videotaped them. On returning to San Francisco, he did the experiment in reverse, asking Americans to link the Fore faces to the stories. Once again, the judgements tallied.

When Ekman first presented his results to the American Anthropological Association, he was met with cries of derision. The cultural theory of emotion was so entrenched that any criticisms were simply laughed out of court. Eventually, however, Ekman won the argument. It is now widely accepted among emotion researchers that some emotions, at least, are not learned, but innate.

Of course, the diehard proponent of the cultural theory of emotion can always retort that Ekman's studies showed only that the facial expressions associated with basic emotions are universal and innate (see Figure 1). The studies tell us nothing about the subjective feelings behind those expressions. This is true enough, but the same applies to everything that is private and subjective. I can never be sure, for example, that your experience of the colour red, or your sense of the sweetness of sugar, are the same as mine. However, if our subjective experiences were really so radically different, it is difficult to know how we could ever communicate at all. We might be able to use the same words in a similarly grammatical fashion, but, if we were using them to represent fundamentally different concepts, we would surely end up in a hopeless muddle of misunderstandings. We would never be able to agree about anything.

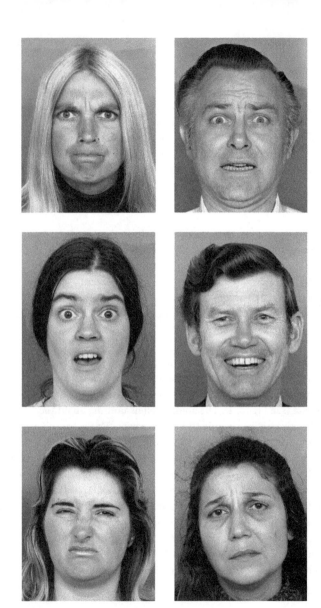

1. Facial expressions of basic emotions.

Now, while disagreement and misunderstanding are certainly common, they are not so common as to prevent all effective communication. Most of us seem to get our message across most of the time. When we read poems and novels written by authors from other cultures, we recognize the emotions they describe. If emotions were cultural inventions, changing as swiftly as language, these texts would seem alien and impenetrable.

Communication is possible without words too. And this is largely thanks to the basic emotions we all share. When anthropologists first come into contact with a previously isolated people, their only means of communication is via facial expressions and bodily gestures, many of which serve to express emotions. The anthropologists may smile, an expression that will be recognized immediately by the isolated tribespeople. The tribespeople may smile in return, showing the anthropologists that they share the same feeling.

Our common emotional heritage binds humanity together, then, in a way that transcends cultural difference. In all places, and at all times, human beings have shared the same basic emotional repertoire. Different cultures have elaborated on this repertoire, exalting different emotions, downgrading others, and embellishing the common feelings with cultural nuances, but these differences are more like those between two interpretations of the same musical work, rather than those between different compositions. Just as two orchestras will play the same symphony slightly differently, so two cultures will play out their emotional repertoire in different tones. It will be clear to all, however, that the score is the same.

The universality of basic emotions argues strongly for their biological nature. If basic emotions were cultural inventions, their ubiquity would be very surprising indeed. If we suppose, however, that they are part of humanity's common biological inheritance, then their presence throughout the world is easy to explain. Just as all human beings have the same kind of body, with minor variations, so we all have the same kind of mind. This universal human nature is encoded in the human genome, the legacy of our shared evolutionary history.

Now that the psychological unity of humankind is more widely acknowledged, it can be hard to understand how the cultural theory of emotion ever gained such widespread acceptance. Perhaps the answer lies in the (equally universal) human tendency to exaggerate the small differences between the various human groups. In the search for cultural identity, we naturally fix on the things that set us apart from others, rather than on the things that link us together. When it comes to emotions, we often pay attention to the small cultural differences, and ignore the overwhelming similarities.

European attitudes to the peoples of South-East Asia are a case in point. For a long time in England and other parts of Europe, people from Japan, China, and countries in South-East Asia were often described as being mysterious and unfathomable. This stereotype of the 'inscrutable oriental' was due in large part to the fact that European travellers found it hard to read their emotions. They wondered whether the poker face of the Japanese might conceal emotions that were very different from their own.

The Japanese do, in fact, take greater pains to hide their emotions than do people in Europe and North America. Every culture has its own rules that define the socially acceptable forms of emotional expression. In Europe and North America, these 'display rules' encourage vivid facial expressions of emotion; a poker face is generally regarded as dull or deceptive. In Japan, on the other hand, excessive emotional displays are often perceived as rude, and Japanese people consequently make more of an effort to attenuate their emotional expressions.

Underneath these display rules, however, the emotions are the same. In an interesting experiment conducted by Paul Ekman and Wallace Friesen, American and Japanese men were videotaped while they watched film clips. Some of the clips were of neutral or pleasant events, such as a canoe trip, while others were of disgusting things such as a ritual circumcision, the suction-aided delivery of a baby, and nasal surgery. In one showing, the subjects watched the clips in private, while in another an interviewer was present. When alone, similar facial expressions were observed in both American and Japanese subjects. When the interviewer was present, however, the Japanese smiled more and showed less disgust than their American counterparts.

The most interesting thing about this experiment, however, became apparent only when the videotapes were viewed in slow motion. Only then was it possible to observe that, when the interviewer was present, the Japanese subjects actually started to make the same expressions of disgust as the Americans did, and succeeded in masking these expressions only a few fractions of a second later. In other words, the same basic emotions were felt by both the Americans and the Japanese. These biological responses were automatic, beyond voluntary control. Only after consciousness caught up, a few hundred milliseconds later, could the learned display rules be imposed on top of the basic biological response.

The inscrutable oriental, then, is concealing not radically different emotions, but the very same emotions as those felt by all other human beings the world over. The European travellers who suspected that an alien mind lurked beneath the less expressive oriental countenance were misled by the superficial differences between their display rules.

As the experiment with the American and Japanese men demonstrates, basic emotions such as fear and disgust are automatic, reflex-like responses over which we have little conscious control. And, like reflexes, they are much faster than anything we do voluntarily. Thus the culturally determined display rules always arrive on the scene after the basic emotional response has been set in motion. The basic emotions are hardwired, etched into our neural circuitry by our genes rather than by our culture, part of the basic mental design that is common to us all.

Higher cognitive emotions

The second group of emotions identified by Paul Griffiths are the higher cognitive emotions. These are not so automatic and fast as basic emotions, and nor are they universally associated with a single facial expression. Love is a case in point. Although love at first sight is possible, it seems much more common for love to grow gradually over the space of several days, weeks, or even months. Contrast this with the emotion of fear, which typically overtakes a person in a matter of milliseconds. And, while fear is easily recognizable by its typical facial expression, there is no specific facial expression associated with the emotion of love.

Higher cognitive emotions involve much more cortical processing than basic emotions. While basic emotions are associated with subcortical structures buried deep below the surface of the brain, emotions like love are more associated with areas of the neocortex. The neocortex is the part of the brain that has expanded most in the past five million years of human evolution and supports most of our most complex cognitive abilities such as explicit logical analysis. The fact that the higher cognitive emotions are more cortical than the basic emotions means that they are more capable of being influenced by conscious thoughts, and this in turn is what allows higher cognitive emotions to be more culturally variable than the basic emotions. However, despite their greater cultural variability, the higher cognitive emotions are still universal. Like basic emotions, the higher cognitive emotions are part of human nature, shaped by our common evolutionary history.

Box 2 Higher cognitive emotions

Higher cognitive emotions are universal, like basic emotions, but they exhibit more cultural variation. They also take longer to build up and longer to die away than basic emotions. Higher cognitive emotions include the following:

- Love
- Guilt
- Shame
- Embarrassment
- Pride
- Envy
- Jealousy

Some basic emotions can also be co-opted for the social functions that typify higher cognitive emotions. When someone feels disgusted by the smell of rotting food, this is a basic emotion. When you feel disgusted by an immoral act, however, the basic emotional response designed to keep you away from infectious or poisonous things is co-opted for the social function of keeping you away from untrustworthy people.

What other higher cognitive emotions are there, besides love? Possible candidates include guilt, shame, embarrassment, pride, envy, and jealousy (see Box 2). This list suggests a further property of higher cognitive emotions: all these emotions are fundamentally social in a way that basic emotions are not. You can be afraid of, or disgusted by, inanimate objects and non-human animals, but love and guilt require other people for their existence. You might feel guilty about hurting an animal, and some people claim to be in love with their pets, but it seems unlikely that guilt and love evolved for such purposes. The higher cognitive emotions seem to have been designed by natural selection precisely to help our ancestors cope with an increasingly complex social environment.

As we will see in Chapter 2, these emotions may be the cement that binds human society together.

Culturally specific emotions

The third and final group of emotions identified by Paul Griffiths are culturally specific emotions. Unlike basic emotions and higher cognitive emotions, these emotions are not universal; they are found in some cultures but not others. The cultural theory of emotion thought this was true of all emotions, but we have seen how this view was overturned by the pioneering work of Paul Ekman. Just because some emotions are universal, however, does not mean that all are.

There is, for example, an emotion felt by the Gururumba people of New Guinea that is apparently not experienced by people from other cultures. It is known as the state of 'being a wild pig', because people who experience it behave just like wild pigs: they run wild, looting articles of small value and attacking bystanders.

This emotion does not appear to be innate. Now, the word 'innate' has been used in lots of quite different ways, and some biologists and philosophers have argued that we should abandon the term altogether. I think the term is fine, so long as we are careful to say what we mean by it. When I say that some trait is 'innate', I mean that it needs very few special conditions for it to develop. In other words, so long as you give a child the basic things it needs to survive, such as food, shelter, and company, that child will develop all the traits that are innate in humans. Language is innate in this sense; you do not need to provide lots of special instruction materials for a child to acquire a language. All you need to do is bring the child up in a group of other humans who can speak. The ability to speak a particular language, such as English or Japanese, is, of course, not innate. Special conditions over and above the basic necessities for survival are required for such a trait to develop. These conditions do not obtain everywhere.

In saying, then, that culturally specific emotions are not innate, all I am saying is that they will not develop unless special conditions are in place, conditions that are provided only by particular cultures. The main such condition is that you learn about this emotion when you are a child. In other words, unlike basic emotions, which develop willy-nilly, culturally specific emotions develop only if you are acquainted with them by your culture. You would never experience the state of being a wild pig unless you observed other people in the grip of this emotion while you were growing up. It is this that distinguishes culturally specific emotions from basic emotions such as fear or anger, which you would have the capacity to feel even if you had never heard of them.

The fact that different cultures can produce human beings with different emotional repertoires is testimony to the remarkable plasticity of the human mind. If you believe that the human mind works in a particular way, then, even if your theory is wildly inaccurate as an account of human psychology in general, your mind may start behaving partly as your theory predicts. In other words, theories about the mind are to some extent self-fulfilling prophecies. If your culture teaches you that there is an emotion called 'being a wild pig', then you will develop the capacity to experience this emotion. And this experience will not be a calculated act of deception. If deception is involved at all, it is a kind of self-deception, though this is probably not a very good way of putting things, as culturally specific emotions do not feel fake. In fact, they *feel* no different from basic emotions, which are universal and innate. Gururumba men—and it is only men who experience this emotion—really feel as if the emotion of 'being a wild pig' has taken them over against their will, in the same way that basic emotions such as fear or disgust just 'happen to us', without any conscious decision on our part. Those in the grip of culturally specific emotions like 'being a wild pig' are not faking it.

An interesting feature of culturally specific emotions like 'being a wild pig' is that they often provide people with a way out of difficult situations. Gururumba men who are in the grip of this emotion are treated with remarkable tolerance; the emotion is seen as an unwelcome but involuntary event, and so people suffering from it are given special consideration, which includes temporary relief from their financial obligations. By a curious coincidence, it so happens that the emotion tends to be experienced by men aged between 25 and 35—precisely the age when they first encounter the financial difficulties that arise in the early years of marriage. How fortunate it is that, just when a man's economic obligations increase, he may experience an emotion that causes others to allow him some leeway in meeting those obligations.

Of course, it is really no coincidence that the state of 'being a wild pig' afflicts just those people who might derive some benefit from it. The psychologist James Averill has argued that it is precisely the function of many emotions that they help people to cope with the particular demands of their culture. If this is true, it is true only of culturally specific emotions. Basic emotions are not tailored to fit the specific demands of a particular culture, but designed to help us meet the fundamental challenges faced by humans everywhere, as we will see in Chapter 2.

Romantic love

What other examples are there of culturally specific emotions? One emotion in particular that has divided opinion is romantic love. Some maintain that it is a universal emotion, hardwired into the brain just like fear and anger. Others disagree, arguing that romantic love is more like the state of 'being a wild pig'. La Rochefoucauld famously declared that 'some people would never have fallen in love if they had never heard of love'. Those who think romantic love is a culturally specific emotion go even further: they claim that nobody would fall in love if they had not previously heard romantic stories.

The most famous proponent of this view was the writer C. S. Lewis, who argued that romantic love was invented in Europe in the early 12th century. It was around this time that 'courtly love' became the central theme of much European poetry. In many of the poems a nobleman would fall in love with a lady at the royal court. He would become her knight and devote himself to her service, though his passion for her would rarely be consummated. The love of Lancelot for King Arthur's wife, Guinevere, is perhaps the best-known story to emerge from this literary genre.

If romantic love really were an invention of some medieval poets, nobody could have felt this emotion before the Middle Ages. Lewis was quite happy to accept this consequence of his provocative thesis and proclaimed that 'no one falls in love in Homer or Virgil'. It is not always clear whether Lewis is talking about literature or psychology—whether he means that poets didn't write about romantic love before the Middle Ages, or whether nobody felt this emotion before then—but there are times when he seems to mean the latter, such as when he states that the emergence of romantic love was one of the few 'real changes in human sentiment' that have ever taken place.

Contrary to Lewis, we might point to texts that long pre-date the medieval poetry of courtly love in which romantic feelings seem unmistakable. A case in point is the Song of Songs, a book in the Old Testament, in which the following verse positively glows with longing:

> What a wound thou hast made, my bride, my true love.
> What a wound thou hast made in this heart of mine!
> And all with one glance of an eye,
> All with one ringlet straying on thy neck!

Anthropologists have also observed romantic love in cultures separated from our own by space as well as time. Yet, if romantic love were a European invention, it could not be experienced by peoples who had had no contact with Europe. This simple consideration allowed two anthropologists to put the cultural theory of romantic love to the test. First, they needed a working definition of romantic love, so they identified the following core features of the idea: a powerful feeling of sexual attraction to a single person, feelings of anguish and longing when the loved one is absent, and intense joy when he or she is present. They also listed other elements, including elaborate courtship gestures such as giving gifts and showing one's love in song and poetry. They then examined the anthropological literature and counted the number of cultures in which this collection of features was described. To their surprise, they found that it was described in 90 per cent of the cultures on record. If anthropologists have actually observed and noted down incidents of romantic love in 90 per cent of the societies they have studied, it is a fair bet that this emotion exists in the remaining 10 per cent too.

This evidence argues strongly for the universality of romantic love. Lewis may still have a point, however. Even if the core elements of romantic love are universal, other aspects may differ from culture to culture to some degree. To return to the musical analogy, the symphony sounds slightly different when played by different orchestras, even though the score is the same. In a similar way, romantic love is played out slightly differently in different cultures. In the West it is marked by special features not found elsewhere. These special features include the idea that romantic love must take you by surprise, the idea that it should be the basis for a lifelong commitment, and the idea that it is the supreme form of self-fulfilment. So, while romantic love is a universal theme, it is a theme that admits of some minor variations.

Complications

The precise roles that biology and culture play in the development of emotions continue to be the subject of lively debate. Some researchers, for example, have questioned the methods used to demonstrate the universality of basic emotions. In many studies, participants are presented with photographs of different facial expressions and asked to match them to words from a given list. But James Russell, a psychologist at Boston University, has argued that providing such prompts artificially inflates identification of the 'correct' emotion. If subjects know that they are trying to identify happiness, sadness, anger, and so on, then that is probably what they will see. When people are asked to come up with their own words, however, they find it much harder to hit the target. In one experiment, removing the list reduced accuracy from over 80 per cent to about 50.

Lisa Feldman Barrett, a psychologist at Northeastern University in Boston, has expanded Russell's critique. She argues that the dogma of universal emotional expressions has been accepted too uncritically and that the data can be explained without it. She suggests that, rather than being biologically based, many emotional expressions are culturally learned symbols—a form of 'body language' that we learn to communicate emotions to others. And, like spoken languages, the expressions share commonalities but also vary from culture to culture. This does not mean that the underlying feelings are culturally specific, but the facial expressions used to convey these feelings may be more culturally variable than Ekman claimed.

Scientific claims are always provisional and the debate about the relative importance of nature and nurture in the development of emotions is ongoing. The criticisms offered by researchers like Russell and Barrett do not invalidate Ekman's theory of basic emotions, but they do suggest ways in which it may need to be refined. The fundamental insight that human emotions have an evolutionary basis remains true. We will explore this idea further in Chapter 2.

Chapter 2
The evolution of emotion

If you have ever seen *Star Trek*, you'll remember Spock, the pointy-eared alien. Spock was half human and half Vulcan—a species that, by some quirk of fate, happened to look remarkably human in all respects other than those tell-tale ears.

The visual similarity, however, concealed a deeper difference. Behind the human-like face lay an alien brain, far superior to ours. In particular, the Vulcan race had learned to suppress their emotions. Having dispensed with these primitive vestiges of their animal origins, the Vulcans were no longer encumbered by passion, and had thereby attained a superhuman degree of rationality.

In supposing that a creature devoid of emotions would be more intelligent than we are, the creators of *Star Trek* were perpetuating an ancient theme of Western culture. Ever since Plato, many Western thinkers have tended to view emotions as obstacles to intelligent action, or, at best, as harmless luxuries. I call this the negative view of emotion.

The opposite idea—the positive view of emotion—is the view that emotions are vital for intelligent action. According to the positive view of emotion, a creature who lacked emotion would be less intelligent than we are, not more. For the past 2,000 years this idea would have struck most Western thinkers as absurd, but considerations drawn from evolutionary theory and neuroscience now argue in its favour.

It is easy to find examples to support the negative view of emotion. We are all familiar with cases in which an excess of emotion prevents people from acting intelligently. A man who is insulted by a gang of hooligans would be safer if he ignored the insult and walked away, but his pride may lead him to answer back and thus become the victim of a violent assault. A woman who is criticized by her boss may become upset and walk out of her job, when the most intelligent response may be to bite her lip and modify her behaviour. And so on.

It would be stupid to deny that emotions can lead people to do things that they later regret. The positive view of emotions does not hold that emotions are always useful. Rather, it maintains that the best recipe for success is a mixture of reason and emotion, not reason alone. Someone who lacked emotions altogether would be better off than us in some circumstances, but worse off in others. Overall, however, the benefits of having emotions outweigh the drawbacks.

The positive view of emotion is supported by evolutionary theory. Emotions are complex traits, and such traits rarely evolve unless they convey some advantage. So the fact that we have emotions now means that, at some point in our evolutionary history at least, they must have helped our ancestors to survive and procreate. The question is—how?

The value of basic emotions

It is easy to see how some of the basic emotions such as fear and anger helped our ancestors to survive. The capacity for fear is clearly useful in a world where hungry predators pose a serious threat. Fear allows animals to react very swiftly to any possible

Box 3 The two routes to fear

The American neuroscientist Joseph LeDoux has found that the fear response is controlled by two separate pathways in the brain. The first of these corresponds to Ekman's basic emotion of fear. It is very quick, but often makes mistakes. The second is slower, but more accurate. Ideally, the two pathways work together to get us the best of both worlds. The first pathway makes us respond quickly to signs of potential danger but can often be set off by false alarms. Meanwhile, the second pathway considers the situation more carefully, and if it concludes that the danger is not real, it cuts off the fear response initiated by the first pathway. In phobias, the second pathway ceases to function properly, so that we continue to react fearfully to harmless stimuli.

sign of danger, pumping their bodies full of hormones that facilitate a fast escape and flooding their minds with one thought: flee! (See Box 3.) Anger is similar, except that it prepares the organism for a fight rather than for flight.

Surprise and disgust are also fairly easy to decipher. The emotion of surprise helps animals to respond to novel stimuli. When something unexpected comes along, the surprise reaction stops us in our tracks and forces us to pay attention to it. Our eyebrows arch, allowing the eyes to widen and take in as much of the new scene as possible. The body readies itself for a possible change in activity. Likewise, the capacity for disgust is helpful in a world where rotting food and faeces are homes to colonies of infectious bacteria. By causing animals to steer clear of such objects, disgust helps them to avoid being poisoned or infected.

The evolutionary rationale for the other two basic emotions—joy and distress—is more complex. They probably evolved to act as motivators leading us to pursue or avoid certain courses of action. We tend to feel joy when we do things that, in the stone age, would have helped us to pass on our genes. The reason why having sex, meeting old friends, and receiving gifts make us joyful is that all these things were conducive to the reproductive success of our ancestors. Conversely, the reason why the death of a friend or the loss of an important possession are so distressing is that these things were bad for the reproductive success of our ancestors. This does not mean that our ancestors made the connection in their minds between these emotions and genetic success. Natural selection did not design our minds to think directly about how best to pass on our genes. Instead, it gave us the capacity to feel joy, and then made the experience of joy contingent on doing the things that help our genes to get into the next generation.

If joy and distress really evolved to function as motivators, like the proverbial carrot and stick, they must work by anticipation. Without an ability to predict whether a particular course of action will lead us to feel joyful or distressed, these emotions could not provide us with a motive for or against taking that course of action. There would be no point in feeling joyful or distressed if we could not use the anticipation of such feelings to help us decide what to do. As we experience such feelings in childhood we gradually learn what things make us joyful or distressed. As we continue to grow up, we use the memory of such feelings to run our lives.

Fortunately, we do not have to rely entirely on our own experience. Although preferences differ from person to person, the fundamental causes of joy and distress are common to us all, so we can learn from other people's experiences too. The same applies to other basic emotions such as fear and disgust. Children who see that their parents are afraid of bathing in a particular river can infer that the river is dangerous without having to test it out for themselves. Likewise, children who see that their parents react with disgust to a particular kind of food can save themselves the trouble of tasting something horrible. In a social species like *Homo sapiens*, then, emotions are doubly useful. On the one hand, the internal feelings and the bodily changes of emotion cause the organism to pursue or avoid particular courses of action. On the other hand, the external expressions of emotion provide information to others, allowing them to learn from our experiences.

The same phenomenon occurs in other social species, including many primates. In one experiment, rhesus macaques reared in a laboratory were unafraid of snakes when they first saw them. However, after watching a film of another monkey reacting to a snake with fear, they too began to show the fear response to snakes. There are limits, however, to this kind of learning from experience. When shown films of other monkeys being frightened by a flower or a rabbit, the laboratory-reared macaques did not develop fears of such harmless things. Emotional learning is a combination of environmental inputs and an innate disposition to learn some things rather than others.

Not all emotional expressions are designed to allow other animals to learn vicariously. Some emotional expressions are not honest signals of the underlying emotion but acts of deception. When a cat is frightened, for example, its fur stands on end. The function of this expression is not to let other animals know that the cat is frightened, however. On the contrary, there are some other animals—predators—that the cat would prefer not to know it was frightened, since that might encourage them to attack. The purpose of the hair standing on end is to make the cat seem bigger than it really is, and hence to deter predators or other cats from attacking.

When considering the evolution of the emotions, then, we must take into consideration all the elements of each emotional response. It is not enough to focus on the internal feelings; we must also consider the facial expressions and other signals.

Darwin was the first to emphasize the importance of these signals, and his book *The Expression of the Emotions in Man and Animals* (1872) examines the continuity of many of them over long stretches of evolutionary time. Darwin was interested in these expressions because he thought they were good evidence that humans had descended from other animals. He argued, for example, that the way our hair stands on end when we are scared is an evolutionary leftover from a time when our ancestors were completely covered in fur. Our ancestors would puff up their fur when scared just like cats do today. Now, of course, a few hairs standing up on our arms are unlikely to make us look much bigger, so the reaction has become much less pronounced, but it is still there nonetheless, a legacy of our pre-human ancestors.

The evolutionary causes of emotional expressions such as hair standing on end in fear, or baring one's teeth in anger, are easy to guess. Other emotional expressions, however, are more mysterious. Tears are a case in point. The question of why we cry when distressed has baffled many evolutionists. Emotional tears are uniquely human. Most mammals have tear glands, but these exist purely to protect the eye against injury. No other species cries when it is distressed—not even our closest relative, the chimpanzee.

Darwin denied that tears shed in distress served any useful function. The tear glands, he argued, evolved as a means of protecting the eyes in infancy, when prolonged screaming might otherwise cause optical damage. Tears shed by adults in distress, thought Darwin, were merely an incidental result of pressure exerted on the tear glands by screwing up the eyes, just as contraction of the same muscles can lead to tears when you laugh or sneeze.

More recently, this view has been challenged by researchers who have proposed a variety of functions for emotional tears. After finding that tears shed in distress have a different biochemical composition from other kinds of tears, William Frey has suggested that such tears remove stress hormones from the body. This, he claims, is the reason why people usually feel better after having had a good cry. A more common view is that tears provide an honest signal of distress. For signals to be honest, they must be hard to fake, and it does indeed seem very difficult to cry on purpose; it takes a lot of practice before actors can do it convincingly. According to this view, the reason we usually feel better after crying has nothing to do with getting rid of excess hormones; it is simply because crying usually prompts other people to offer us their support. One problem with this theory, however, is that it does not explain why crying on your own can sometimes make you feel better.

As humans are the only animals that cry when distressed, this particular emotional expression must have evolved after the human lineage diverged from the chimpanzee lineage. Most other emotional expressions are much older. The tendency for our hair to stand on end when we are afraid probably originated over fifty million years ago, when the common ancestor of mammals prowled the earth. The emotion of fear itself is even older than this particular physiological expression. In fact, fear is probably one of the first emotions ever to have evolved. It is likely to have been present in the first vertebrates, which appeared some 500 million years ago or more. All animals descended from these early vertebrates—amphibians, reptiles, birds, and mammals—have inherited the capacity for fear. Humans are far from unique in this respect.

Other basic emotions such as joy and distress may have come later, but they are still very old, and thus shared by many animals other than humans. Who can doubt that a cat curled up by a warm fire is feeling its own kind of joy when it purrs so loudly? Evidence for the capacity of non-human animals to feel distress is harder to come by, but it is difficult to resist the impression that elephants, at least, feel this emotion. Mother elephants are often reluctant to abandon the corpses of their children when they have been slain by hunters, despite the danger this puts them in, and they often return to the proverbial elephants' graveyard.

Before you accuse me of sentimentality, consider the evidence from neuroanatomy. When you compare the brains of widely differing animals, the similarities are striking. In all vertebrates, for example, the brain is divided into three distinct parts known as the hindbrain, midbrain, and forebrain, and within each of these divisions one can find the same basic structures and pathways. This shows that brain evolution is a very conservative process, in which many systems undergo remarkably little modification even though the rest of the body might change dramatically.

This is especially clear with the brain structures associated with fear and anger. In all mammals, including ourselves, fear and anger are mediated by a set of neural structures known as the limbic system. These include the hippocampus, the cingulate gyrus, the anterior thalamus, and the amygdala (see Figure 2). All these structures are tucked away in the centre of the brain, underneath the outer layer of neural tissue known as the neocortex. The neocortex is, in evolutionary terms, much more recent than the limbic system. While there is a kind of neocortex in the brains of fish, amphibians, birds, and reptiles, in mammals it is very much larger and completely envelops the limbic structures. The much larger neocortex is, indeed, the main difference between the brains of mammals and those of other vertebrates. According to the neuroscientist Paul MacLean, the evolution of the mammalian brain involved the expansion of the neocortex, while the older limbic structures were much less modified, though of course the latter did not remain exactly the same. In making these cross-species comparisons, everything is a question of degree; my limbic structures are different from those of a chimp (I hope), but the chimp's brain and mine are quite similar when compared to the brain of a fish.

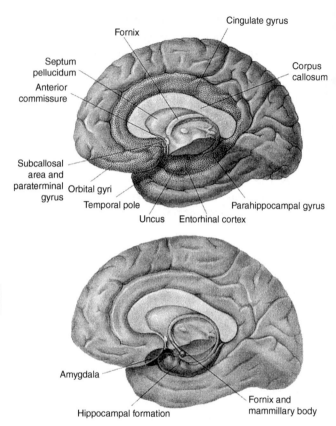

2. **Location of the hippocampus and amygdala and surrounding cortical areas.**

If basic emotions like fear are mediated exclusively by the limbic system, the higher cognitive emotions such as love and guilt seem to involve much more cortical processing. This would suggest that they evolved much later than basic emotions, long after the point when the neocortex began to expand with the emergence of the higher mammals. In other words, higher cognitive emotions might be no more than sixty million years old, which is very young compared to the 500 or so million years for which the vertebrate brain—and the basic emotions—have been around. In fact, they may well be even more recent than that.

The evolution of guilt, love, and revenge

If the time when higher cognitive emotions such as guilt and love first evolved is still unclear, the reason *why* they evolved is even more obscure. It is easy to see how the capacity for fear or disgust helped our ancestors to survive, but it is harder to understand what benefits they gained by falling in love or feeling guilty. Yet a number of intriguing suggestions have been put forward that might explain why these emotions too are useful. These suggestions are still largely speculative but they do provide some further insights into the possible benefits of having emotions.

Guilt is a case in point. On the face of it, it is hard to see why natural selection would have endowed us with this emotion. There are many occasions in life when it is possible to cheat—to take a benefit without paying the corresponding price. If you can cheat without being detected, the most advantageous thing to do is surely to cheat. If you have a conscience, however, the thought of the guilt that you would feel afterwards might prevent you from cheating. Thus it seems that an animal with the capacity for guilt would be outcompeted by less scrupulous rivals. The capacity for guilt would be eliminated by natural selection.

This analysis has been challenged by the economist Robert Frank. Frank argues that it is advantageous to have the capacity for guilt because people who are known to have a conscience are more likely to be trusted by others. He tells the following story to illustrate his point. Consider two people, Smith and Jones, who wish to start a restaurant. Smith is a talented cook and Jones is a shrewd manager, so together they can launch a successful joint venture that pays each of them more than they would gain from working alone. Yet each of them knows that the other will have opportunities to cheat without being detected. Smith can take kickbacks from food suppliers, for example, while Jones can fiddle the accounts. If only one of them cheats, he will do very well, while the other does poorly. But if both of them cheat, each will do worse than they would do if both were honest. If Smith and Jones could each make a binding commitment not to cheat, both would profit by doing so. But how can they make such a commitment in a way that is credible? Simply promising not to cheat is not convincing; for unscrupulous people, promises are easy to make and just as easy to break.

Here is where guilt comes in handy. If you feel guilty whenever you cheat, this can lead you to behave honestly even when you know that you could get away with cheating. And if others know that you are this kind of person, they will seek you out as a partner in joint ventures that require trust. This depends, of course, on there being reliable cues that indicate the presence of guilt. Only if there is some reliable signal that you have a conscience, such as blushing when you feel guilty, will others be able to tell the difference between a trustworthy person and a scoundrel. These signals must be hard to fake, otherwise they would not be reliable. Frank argues that some emotional expressions, such as blushing, have been built into human physiology by natural selection precisely to serve as such reliable signals of trustworthiness.

There are lots of other situations in life when it is vital to be able to make credible promises. Frank refers to all these situations as 'commitment problems' and argues that all the higher cognitive emotions solve different kinds of commitment problem. The capacity for guilt solves those commitment problems in which you have to make a credible promise not to cheat. Likewise, argues Frank, romantic love solves another kind of commitment problem—that in which you have to make a credible promise to remain faithful to one other person. Jack and Jill may consider each other suitable mates, but they will be reluctant to commit themselves to each other unless each is sure that the other will not walk out as soon as someone more attractive comes along. The realization that the other person is in love can provide this assurance. If Jack commits himself to Jill because of an emotion he did not 'decide' to have (and so cannot decide *not* to have), an emotion that is reliably indicated by such physiological signals as a racing heart and difficulty in sleeping, then Jill will be more likely to believe he will stay with her than if he had chosen her after coolly weighing up her good and bad points. 'People who are sensible about love are incapable of it,' wrote Douglas Yates.

Another commitment problem involves making credible threats of retaliation. Suppose you are the smallest child in the class, and the class bully threatens to steal your lunch. You might threaten to retaliate by punching the bully on the nose, but, if the bully knows you are a rational person, he will not take your threat very seriously. After all, punching the bully on the nose will probably lead to a fight that you will almost certainly lose, and you would then be even worse off, having lost your lunch as well as gaining a black eye or two. If, however, you have a reputation for vengeance, your problem is solved. The impulse to seek revenge will cause you to retaliate after insults regardless of the consequences, so the bully will think twice about stealing your sandwiches. Once again, emotions seem to exhibit a kind of 'global rationality' that saves pure reason from itself.

According to Frank, then, higher cognitive emotions such as guilt, love, and revenge perform very useful functions. They help us to solve commitment problems that we would be incapable of solving by reason alone. However, these emotions are not without their disadvantages. They may help us to make credible promises and threats, but what if someone calls our bluff? If, despite my racing pulse and reddening face, my declarations of love fall on deaf ears, I will be condemned to several weeks, months, or perhaps even years of useless suffering. Unrequited love is surely one of nature's cruellest punishments. Likewise, if the school bully goes ahead and steals my sandwiches despite being aware of my taste for vengeance, my retaliation will lead me to be even worse off than before, losing my sandwiches and acquiring a nasty bruise.

It would be nice, of course, if we could obtain the benefits of these emotions without incurring the dangers that ensue when someone calls our bluff. It would be great, for example, if the pangs of love could suddenly vanish whenever our advances were spurned. Or if we could make credible threats of retaliation that melted into timidity whenever someone decided to take us at our word. But to behave in this way would undermine the credibility of any promises and threats we might make in the future. To make a credible threat, you must show that you are somehow forced to carry it out. It seems that the higher cognitive emotions cannot avoid being double-edged swords.

Promises and threats are credible only if there is some evidence that you will carry them out even if it costs you to do so. You must show that you are 'handcuffed' in some way to the execution of the threat or promise. Let us call this the 'handcuff principle'. For emotions to work, in other words, they must have a kind of inevitability built into them, such that, when someone calls your bluff, you cannot avoid carrying out your promise or threat. These emotions handcuff you to a particular course of action that you would rather not carry out.

Furthermore, this handcuff must be clearly visible to others. There is no point in having such a mechanism if others cannot see it. In the case of guilt, the handcuff is visibly indicated by physiological cues such as blushing. Most of the time, one hopes, the visibility of the handcuff deters people from calling your bluff. The school bully sees that you are prey to bouts of righteous anger and leaves your sandwiches alone. But, occasionally, the deterrent fails. The bully steals your sandwiches anyway, leaving you with no option but to take revenge. The desire for revenge then kicks in, impelling you to punch the bully on the nose. The voice of reason, calling for caution, is swamped by the tide of passion.

When both parties in a dispute are each handcuffed in the same way, another danger arises. In such situations, it needs only one party to call the other's bluff to set off a potentially never-ending cycle of tit for tat. Steven Pinker tells a parable that illustrates this danger. By a fortuitous coincidence, it involves some real handcuffs:

> Protesters attempt to block the construction of a nuclear power plant by lying down on the railroad tracks leading to the site. The engineer, being reasonable, has no choice but to stop the train. The railroad company counters by telling the engineer to set the throttle so that the train moves very slowly and then to jump out of the train and walk beside it. The protesters must scramble. Next time the protesters handcuff themselves to the tracks; the engineer does not dare leave the train. But the protesters must be certain the engineer sees them in enough time to stop. The company assigns the next train to a near-sighted engineer.

It is this unfortunate logic that lies behind the eternal vendettas between Mafia families in Italy and the tit-for-tat sectarian murders in some parts of the Middle East. Wherever the force of law is weak, self-perpetuating cycles of attack and revenge are common. They persist even though they are clearly not in the interest of either party, simply because the impulse to seek revenge is etched deep into our biology. As we have seen, there is a good evolutionary reason for this unfortunate feature of human nature. Without a taste for revenge, we would be easy to exploit.

Are emotions still useful today?

What about now, though? Emotions such as the taste for revenge may have been useful to our hunter-gatherer ancestors, whose vendettas were conducted with sticks and stones and led to far fewer fatalities, but they are surely counterproductive in a world in which guns are freely available. Perhaps all emotions are like this. Perhaps the Vulcan race really is ahead of us in the evolutionary game. Spock and his fellow Vulcans may have done well to leave their emotions behind them when their world became high tech.

This seems to have been Darwin's view, whose book on the expression of the emotions gives the impression that these expressions, while useful in the past, are no longer of any value. In arguing, for example, that the tendency for humans to bare their teeth in anger was a leftover from primitive displays of aggression in our pre-human ancestors, Darwin seems to imply that it is rather like the appendix—a vestigial organ, derived from an earlier phase of our evolutionary history, which is no longer of any use.

It is true that we live in a world that is very different, in many ways, from the world in which our ancestors lived. We no longer face the constant threat of being eaten by predators, for example, and the chance of being assaulted by other humans is surely much reduced. If the emotion of fear evolved to help us avoid these dangers, then it might seem that we would be better off without it today. Certainly, an excessive capacity for fear leads to all sorts of problems that many people would dearly love to be free of, such as phobias and panic attacks. One does not hear of many people who suffer from the opposite problem—that of having too little fear. The reason for this apparent imbalance, however, may well be that those with no capacity for fear end up in the morgue long before they are aware they have a problem. Fear does not merely protect us against predators. It also deters us from a whole host of reckless behaviours, many of which are potentially fatal. Fear will stop you from crossing a busy road without looking, or from dancing on the edge of a cliff. A life without fear might be less painful, but it would also be a lot shorter.

Anger, too, might seem to be rather useless today. Unlike our pre-human ancestors, most of us do not regularly engage in physical violence, so what is the benefit of conserving an emotional capacity whose function is to help us fight? One answer is that fighting need not be a physical affair. Our disputes are carried on by other means today, but they still require grit and determination. People who never get angry never get ahead. Moreover, we should not exaggerate the degree to which the need for physical violence has disappeared from our world. There are still many times, even in the affluent and law-abiding cultures of the developed world, when resorting to physical violence is the only way to defend oneself. The film *Demolition Man* is set in the future, at a time when the human capacity for anger has completely atrophied. When a vicious criminal appears on the scene, resuscitated from the state of suspended animation to which he was condemned in the 20th century, nobody is able to deal with him. The criminal is caught only following the revival of another 20th-century human, a policeman who, like the criminal, still possesses the capacity for anger.

If a deficit of anger can be problematic, so too can an excess. Road rage is an obvious example. Worn down by the stress of driving on increasingly crowded roads, some drivers reach a point where the smallest annoyance causes them to snap. Sometimes a frustrated driver simply sounds his horn or swears at the person who has annoyed him. At other times, however, he may jump out of his car and drag the other driver from his seat into the road, where he vents his frustration by punching and kicking him. Anger is useful in the right amount, but when it is excessive it can lead to serious problems.

The same point applies to many other emotions. Even sexual jealousy may have an optimal midpoint between extreme possessiveness and extreme permissiveness (see Box 4). The optimal state of an emotion involves having just the right amount of it, neither too little nor too much. Aristotle based his whole ethical system around this simple idea. The virtues, in his theory, are midpoints between the extremes of having too little or too much of a particular emotion. Courage is the midpoint between

Box 4 Jealousy: good or bad?

Like other higher cognitive emotions, sexual jealousy evolved to help our ancestors survive and reproduce in complex social groups. By prompting them to keep a watchful eye over their mates, jealousy helped our ancestors to make sure that their sexual partners were not defaulting on the cooperative venture of having and raising children. As with other emotions, however, too much can be a bad thing. Too much jealousy can lead people to be violent and coercive, which can drive the partner away or even result in his or her death. Stalkers are usually jilted lovers whose jealousy leads them to pursue their former partners with inappropriate and frightening zeal. Such examples of jealousy gone wrong can easily tempt us into thinking that all jealousy is bad. This is to throw the baby out with the bath water. Too much jealousy is a bad thing, but so is too little. How many people would feel their partner truly loved them if they never showed any signs of jealousy?

too much and too little fear. The virtue of amiability lies halfway between the extremes of cantankerousness and obsequiousness. And so on.

Aristotle's concept of the golden mean is remarkably similar to what psychologists now refer to as 'emotional intelligence'. Emotional intelligence involves striking a balance between emotion and reason in which neither is completely in control. Emotionally intelligent people know when it is right to control their emotions and when it is right to be controlled by them.

Emotional intelligence also involves the ability to read other people's emotions correctly. Guessing other people's emotional state is easy when they are in fits of tears, but the signs are not always so obvious. We often try to mask our emotions, making it harder for others to guess what we are feeling, though we rarely succeed in controlling all the involuntary twitches that betray our inner thoughts. The capacity to gauge someone's mood from such subtle signs is a much rarer talent, though it can be improved with practice.

Evidence is now mounting that the ability to recognize facial expressions of emotion is associated with specialized neural circuitry. These circuits comprise key limbic structures such as the amygdala. When these structures are damaged, the circuit is broken and the ability to discriminate between different facial expressions of emotion is diminished. Bilateral damage to the amygdala, for example, reduces people's ability to detect negative emotions such as fear and anger. It seems that evolution did not just shape our capacity to feel and express emotions, but also gave us special-purpose mechanisms for emotional recognition.

The usefulness of such neural machinery should be clear by now. Without the ability to identify the emotions felt by others, we would lose many opportunities to learn from their experience, with the result that we would have to learn everything the hard way—on our own. We would also find it much harder to know whom to trust. Involuntary emotional signals provide some of the most reliable information about people's characters. In one experiment, strangers were paired at random and given thirty minutes to talk with each other. Then they were asked to make a simple decision, in private, about whether or not they would cooperate with the other person, or cheat. They were also asked to guess what the other person would do. Success rates were remarkably high. The subjects of these experiments all had normal brains; those whose ability to detect emotional cues has been diminished by brain-damage do much worse in similar experimental conditions.

It should be clear by now that a person who lacked emotions would not survive for very long. Lacking fear, he might sit around and ponder whether or not the approaching lion really represented a threat or not. Without anger, she would be picked on mercilessly. Without the capacity to feel disgust, he might be tempted to consume faeces and rotting food. And without the capacity for joy and distress, she might never bother doing anything at all—not a good recipe for survival. *Star Trek* notwithstanding, the Vulcan race could never have evolved.

Moral sentiments

A person without emotions would not just die sooner; they probably wouldn't be very nice either. Emotions seem to pervade much of our moral lives. A long line of thinkers, from Aristotle to Adam Smith, have emphasized the fundamental role of emotion in guiding ethical behaviour. I have already mentioned Aristotle's concept of virtue as a midpoint between emotional extremes. Adam Smith also linked emotions to morality, though in a rather different way. He thought that some emotions were designed specifically for the purpose of helping us to behave morally, a view that now seems to be supported by evolutionary theory. Smith referred to these emotions as 'the moral sentiments'.

Other thinkers have taken a very different view of the relationship between emotion and morality. Hobbes thought that our natural emotional inclinations would almost always make us tend towards selfish behaviour and that the only way to behave in a moral fashion was to transcend our animal instincts and act in accordance with the law. A similar view was proposed by Kant. Kant did not deny that emotions could sometimes lead us to do the right thing, but he argued that such emotionally inspired actions were not truly virtuous. If a man obeyed the moral law out of fear, for example, he could not be called truly virtuous. The only way of behaving morally, according to Kant's view, was to obey the moral law completely unemotionally, purely for the sake of obeying the law.

This strikes me as a bloodless view of morality fit only for Vulcans. Unfortunately, however, Kant's Vulcan morality has had a great deal of influence on Western thought. On the one hand, it has encouraged a negative view of emotion, so that it is now common to think that acts lose their moral worth when they are inspired by emotion. A classic example of this perverse reasoning was provided by a Conservative politician a few years ago in England. In an attempt to discredit the policies of the Opposition, which aimed at redistributing wealth more equitably among all layers of society, he accused his opponents of preaching 'the politics of envy'. The implicit reasoning is clear: envy is an emotion, and not a very nice one at that, so any policy motivated by it must be similarly bad. But envy is not all bad. In fact, it may prove to be crucial for our sense of justice and for motivating us to build a fairer society; 'envy is the basis of democracy,' wrote Bertrand Russell. It may well have evolved precisely for such purposes, as a means to prevent excessive inequality during the long period when our ancestors lived in small bands of hunter-gatherers. Or it may simply have evolved to motivate people to get more for themselves. Either way, envy is part of human nature, and the politicians cannot legislate it out of existence. All we can do is decide how we express it; either through policies of wealth redistribution, or through violence and theft.

On the other hand, the Kantian view of morality has also given rise to a misleading view of how people make moral decisions. According to a view known as moral law theory, whenever we have to decide which course of action is morally superior, we do so by applying a set of general rules to a particular situation, just as we solve a mathematical equation. Ideas like this prompted the philosopher Leibniz to dream about creating a machine that would apply the rules for you, thereby automating all moral decisions and finally removing all uncertainty from our moral life. If we wanted to know whether something was right or wrong, all we would need to do would be to consult our moral computer.

The fantasy of the moral algorithm still underlies a lot of work in the psychology of moral behaviour today. Theories of how the capacity for moral reasoning develops in children are still largely based on the idea that such development consists in acquiring a set of rules. *Star Trek*, once again, provides us with a personification of this idea, though this time the character is from *Star Trek: The Next Generation* rather than from the original series. Commander Data is an android, a robot so human-like that it is hard to tell the difference between him and us. Inside Data's silicon brain is a specialized bit of software concerned exclusively with moral behaviour. In one episode, this 'ethical subroutine' was disabled, and Data suddenly became inconsiderate and then psychopathic.

Psychopaths are indeed curiously amoral, but this is not because they lack an 'ethical subroutine'. The moral capacities that most of us have, and that psychopaths lack, are not based on a set of rules like the instructions in a computer program, but on emotions like sympathy, guilt, and pride. The development of moral capacities in children is, therefore, not likely to be helped by teaching them a set of commandments or precepts, unless their emotional capacities are also well nurtured. Psychopaths are only too good at applying rules. Without moral sentiments to guide your moral reasoning, you would only ever obey the letter of the law rather than the spirit.

The role of emotions in morality is an active and ongoing area of research. Some of the most interesting research in this area concerns shame, guilt, embarrassment, and pride. These are all 'self-conscious emotions', in the sense that they are evoked by self-reflection and self-evaluation. This self-evaluation need not be explicit and conscious; it can also be non-verbal and below conscious awareness. Either way, the self is the object of these emotions.

Many people use the terms 'shame' and 'guilt' synonymously, but contemporary researchers often attempt to distinguish one from the other. Research consistently shows that shame and guilt lead to different kinds of behaviour. Shame leads people to deny, hide, or escape the shame-inducing situation, while guilt leads people to confess, apologise, and repair the consequences of their misdeeds. Guilt thus appears to be the more adaptive emotion, benefiting individuals and their relationships, while shame can often be harmful to both the person who experiences it and those around them. In particular, victims of sexual abuse are often haunted by feelings of shame that can lead to depression and post-traumatic stress disorder.

Researchers investigating the role of emotions in morality do not just focus on unpleasant emotions like guilt and shame. They also study pleasant feelings such as pride, elevation, and gratitude. A variety of experimental findings suggest that feelings of gratitude can enhance psychological resilience, physical health, and the quality of daily life. So while it may be nice when someone thanks you, they may benefit even more from their expression of gratitude than you do.

The psychology of positive emotions is an active area of contemporary research. In Chapter 3 we will explore some of the main findings in the psychology of happiness.

Chapter 3
How to be happy

The range of things that can make us joyful or distressed is simply vast. Witnessing a beautiful sunset, making love, eating an ice cream, and listening to Bach's cantatas are four very different kinds of activity, but they are all capable of inducing joy. On the downside, losing your favourite teddy bear, failing an exam, and hearing about the death of a loved one can all provoke distress. Is there any pattern underlying this bewildering diversity?

In an attempt to answer this question, psychologists have compiled a huge database on what makes people happy. Happiness is not the same as joy, but it is closely linked. Joy is a basic emotion, and, like the other basic emotions, a single episode lasts only a few seconds, rarely more than a minute. Happiness is a mood, and moods last much longer—from several minutes to several hours. Moods are background states that raise or lower our susceptibility to emotional stimuli. In a happy mood, for example, we will be more likely to react joyfully to good news, while, in a sad mood, we might not react so intensely. Conversely, someone in a sad mood is more likely to cry at bad news, while a person in a happy mood might laugh it off. In an anxious mood, we are more easily frightened, while an irritable mood makes us more readily angered.

Happiness is more important than joy because happiness lasts longer and makes joy more likely. The joy produced by witnessing a beautiful sunset is fleeting, but the experience may put us in a happy mood that stays with us for hours. When psychologists do research on general life satisfaction, they are investigating happiness, not joy. The World Database of Happiness combines the results of hundreds of surveys that have been carried out on life satisfaction.

Combing through this database, the first thing that leaps out is that material wealth is not a surefire route to happiness. The old cliché about the impossibility of buying contentment seems to be borne out by the scientific research. Of course, a certain amount of money can help to protect you from some of the most common causes of unhappiness, such as starvation and lack of medical care, but there is more to a happy life than simply avoiding pain and hunger.

Many people today, however, cling to the illusion that gaining material wealth will be the key to all their problems. Hence the common dream of winning the lottery. Such dreams might not be so common if people knew about the studies that have been done on people who really have won lots of money. These studies reveal that winning the lottery does not lead to lasting happiness. When people win a fortune on the lottery, a few find that their life satisfaction increases, but in most cases the euphoria quickly wears off and the winners feel exactly as they did before. Those who were happy beforehand return to their state of normal happiness. Those who were depressed go back to being depressed.

Getting rich quickly rarely leads to long-term bliss in itself. When the initial high has worn off, you may even be less happy than before. This, at least, was what Adam Smith thought (see Box 5), although some recent research casts doubt on this idea. Smith argued that sudden good fortune, monetary or otherwise, was likely to backfire. The story of Johnny Ace is a case in point. Johnny Ace was a rock-'n'-roll star who shot to fame when his first

Box 5 Adam Smith on the perils of good fortune

'The man who, by some sudden revolution of fortune, is lifted up at once into a condition of life, greatly above what he had formerly lived in, may be assured that the congratulations of his best friends are not all of them perfectly sincere. An upstart, though of the greatest merit, is generally disagreeable, and a sentiment of envy commonly prevents us from heartily sympathising with his joy. If he has any judgement, he is sensible of this, and instead of appearing to be elated with his good fortune, he endeavours, as much as he can, to smother his joy...It is seldom that with all of this he succeeds. We suspect the sincerity of his humility, and he grows weary of this constraint. In a little time, therefore, he generally leaves all of his old friends behind him, some of the meanest among them excepted, who may, perhaps, condescend to become his dependents: nor does he always acquire any new ones; the pride of his new connections is as much affronted by finding him their equal, as that of his old ones had been by his becoming their superior: and it requires the most obstinate and persevering modesty to atone for this mortification to either. He generally grows weary too soon, and is provoked, by the sullen and suspicious pride of the one, and by the saucy contempt of the other, to treat the first with neglect, and the second with petulance, till at last he grows habitually insolent, and forfeits the esteem of all. If the chief part of human happiness arises from the consciousness of being beloved, as I believe it does, those sudden changes of fortune seldom contribute much to happiness. He is happiest who advances more gradually to greatness...'

Source: Adam Smith, *The Theory of Moral Sentiments* (1759)

single reached number one in 1952. His next three records were all instant hits too. Suddenly, this obscure preacher's son had become a rock star. Then his luck ran out. His fifth single did well, but not as well as the previous ones. His sixth record did not even get into the charts. On Christmas Eve 1954, Johnny put a revolver to his head and blew his brains out. According to one account, he was just clowning about with the gun. It seems more likely, however, that the sudden rise to fame left him ill prepared for the setbacks that most other musicians get used to dealing with early on in their careers.

If material wealth and sudden good fortune do not lead to happiness, what does? According to the happiness database, the things that are most likely to make you happy are good health, good friends, and, above all, good family relationships. Getting on well with parents, children, and partners is the key to a happy life. A stable loving relationship is far more likely to bring lasting joy than winning the lottery. Once again, the old clichés are remarkably accurate.

If happiness is mostly about getting and keeping good relationships, sadness is linked with failing to achieve good relationships and losing them. Losing a lot of money will make you sad but losing a loved one will make you even sadder. If sadness is about loss, the most painful losses involve people rather than things: the moment when a child leaves home, the betrayal of a friendship, the death of a partner.

In Chapter 2 we saw that the emotions of joy and distress evolved to act as motivators, like an internal carrot and stick. The moods of happiness and sadness may work in a similar way. Natural selection did not design our minds to think directly about how best to pass on our genes. Instead, it gave us the capacity to feel happy, and then it made the experience of happiness contingent on doing the things that help our genes to get into the next generation. The reason that falling in love makes us happy is that those of our ancestors who liked falling in love were more likely to pass on their genes than those who preferred solitude.

This works only if the things that make us happy are also the things that assist genetic replication. For millions of years, this was the case. In the stone age and before, the only way for our ancestors to be happy was by doing the things that helped them to pass on their genes, such as having friends and lovers. In the past few thousand years, however, the development of technology has changed all that. Alone among all animal species, humans have invented artificial means of inducing pleasurable moods and avoiding unpleasant ones. These technologies of mood short-circuit the routes to happiness designed by natural selection. Instead of wasting months or years looking for a romantic partner, we can get an instant high by taking a drug. In order to be happy, we no longer need to do the things that help us pass on our genes. It appears we have outsmarted natural selection.

Talkin' blues

The first technology of mood our ancestors discovered was language. People have used language in various ways to induce happiness artificially, ways that offer no obvious genetic benefits. I will mention three: consoling, entertaining, and 'venting'. The first two methods benefit the hearer; the last is supposed to benefit the speaker.

Our ancestors must have consoled each other with hugs and caresses long before they learned how to talk, but once language was invented they found a new way of providing consolation by offering words of sympathy and advice. In doing so, they discovered that words can be powerful antidepressants. This practice has been around for so long that it now appears almost instinctual. Faced with friends who are feeling down, we all naturally find ourselves trying to talk them out of it. We also naturally administer the same linguistic medicine to ourselves, whispering silent words of encouragement in our minds when we are low. Cognitive therapy, a form of psychotherapy pioneered by Aaron Beck in the 1960s, is based on just this kind of internal monologue. While cognitive therapy may be original in the way it tries to formalize this process, the practice of talking oneself up is probably as old as language itself.

By teaching people to identify their negative thoughts and replace them with more positive ones, cognitive therapists hope to allow people to become the masters of their emotions rather than their slaves. The idea behind this is an old one, going at least as far back as the Stoics, whom we met in Chapter 1. The Stoics observed that emotions both influence, and are influenced by, the thoughts we have (more on this in Chapter 4). By training ourselves to eliminate thoughts that provoke bad moods and to encourage thoughts that foster pleasant emotions, we may be able to gain some measure of control over our emotional state and lift ourselves out of the blues by sheer will power. But this may not always be possible. Sometimes, the intensity of the emotion may not permit alternative thoughts to be entertained, which is why cognitive therapy may not always work for someone in the grip of a severe depression. Nevertheless, when administered by a trained therapist, cognitive therapy can be as effective in treating depression as drugs like Prozac.

Another way of using language to cheer someone up is by telling stories and jokes. Stories appeal to our evolved appetite for social information, but manage to satisfy that appetite despite the fact that they are untrue. This is rather odd from an evolutionary point of view. If language evolved, as some people have argued, to enable our ancestors to swap information about other members of the social group, then we should expect the emotional satisfaction that arises from obtaining such information to be contingent on believing it to be true. There are not many evolutionary advantages to be gained from pursuing and taking delight in false information. Yet this is exactly what seems to underlie the universal human love of fiction and drama. The evolutionary benefits of our sense of humour, to which jokes appeal, are even more mysterious. The psychologist Geoffrey Miller proposes that stories and jokes delight us because they do, in fact, provide useful information—information about the intelligence of the narrator. When someone makes up a story, he is calling attention to his own creativity. When someone tells us a joke, he is displaying his understanding of what makes others laugh. So perhaps telling stories and jokes are not really technologies either, but instincts.

A third linguistic technology of emotion is venting. Venting means talking about unpleasant emotions in order to make them go away. Unlike consolation and entertainment, which may be as old as language itself, venting may be a relatively recent invention. People have probably used language to 'get things off their chest' for thousands of years, but venting is more than just unburdening yourself of a troublesome thought. It is the use of language for the explicit purpose of getting rid of unpleasant emotions. The idea of venting was largely pioneered by the Viennese physician Sigmund Freud (1859–1939), who argued that speaking about negative emotions was sometimes the only way to be rid of them. To understand how Freud arrived at this view, it is necessary to digress a little and look at the 'hydraulic theory' of emotion on which Freud's arguments seem to rest.

Hydraulics is the science of conveying liquids through pipes and channels, and the hydraulic theory of emotion views feelings as mental fluids that circulate around the mind, much as the blood courses through the veins. Whenever you hear someone telling you not to 'bottle your feelings up' or warning you that you will 'burst under pressure', they are implicitly endorsing this view. As some liquids can easily be converted into vapours, gaseous metaphors such as 'letting off steam' can also be pressed into the service of the hydraulic theory.

The hydraulic theory of emotion goes back at least as far as the French philosopher and scientist René Descartes (1596–1650). Descartes envisaged the nerves as pneumatic pipes, transmitting the pressure of 'animal spirits' from nerve endings to the brain, and thence to the muscles. This was very much in line with humoral theory, which dominated medical thinking in the West from the time of the Greeks until the 18th century. According to this theory, the most important determinants of health were the four 'humours' found in the body: blood, phlegm, black bile, and yellow bile. Most illnesses were thought to result from imbalances or blockages in these liquids.

In Freud's work, the humoral metaphor is applied to mental disorder. Freud argued that, since the mind was constantly being replenished with a kind of mental fluid, the libido, it could also be subject to blockages. Such blockages meant that the mental fluid could not be discharged via the normal route emotional expression, and therefore seek discharge via other, more dangerous outlets, such as psychosomatic symptoms. In other words, the inhibition of natural emotional expressions could lead to dangerous consequences. If you are angry and you do not vent the anger directly, it will not just go away. If the anger is not discharged via its natural outlet, such as shouting at the person who annoyed you, it will well up inside you like some noxious fluid and lead to mental illness. Luckily, argued Freud, there were other ways to 'get it out of your system', such as talking to a psychotherapist; this would allow a dangerous build-up of emotion to be vented without transgressing social norms or making yourself ill.

The idea that talking about your feelings functions as a kind of safety valve, allowing psychic pressure to be vented just as excess steam is allowed to escape from a blocked pipe, is sometimes referred to as the 'cathartic theory' of emotion. Anything that allows you to 'get it out of your system' is called a 'cathartic' experience. Catharsis is a Greek term, and plays a central role in

Aristotle's *Poetics*, but the word had a very different meaning then. It certainly had nothing to do with the hydraulic theory of emotion. The current usage of the term goes back to Freud, who used it to describe the discharge of his hypothetical 'mental fluid'. In so doing, Freud unwittingly fostered the mistaken belief that the hydraulic theory of emotion goes back to Ancient Greece. Nothing could be further from the truth. There is still some dispute about what exactly Aristotle meant by catharsis, but we know that it was not about 'letting off steam'. The philosopher Martha Nussbaum has argued that Aristotle thought of catharsis as an intellectual activity, in which the relation of emotions to human action was clarified by a process of experience and reflection. According to Aristotle, the theatre was the perfect place to practise catharsis, perhaps because it allows us to experience emotions at what the sociologist Thomas Scheff has called 'a best aesthetic distance'. If we are caught up directly in a powerful emotion, it may be too overwhelming for us to learn from the experience. Conversely, if we are too distant from an emotional event, it will not touch us at all. The function of drama may be to provide us with a context in which emotions may be experienced at a safe distance so that we may learn how to deal with them better in the future.

So, if the hydraulic theory of emotion is not an Ancient Greek idea, and has little to do with Aristotle's idea of catharsis, where does it come from? As already noted, it has elements that can be traced back to the humoral theory of disease and Descartes's view of nerves as pneumatic pumps. However, the idea that the verbal expression of emotion functions like a safety valve is much more recent. Since Freud popularized the idea at the beginning of the 20th century, it has grown in popularity until it is now common currency in many Western countries. We look back at the stiff-necked Victorians with a smug sense of superiority. 'Emotional literacy' is held in high esteem. People who cannot talk openly about their feelings are regarded as psychologically immature, relics of a bygone age when repression reigned supreme. However, psychologists are increasingly realizing that the hydraulic theory of emotion is too simplistic. It may well be very good on some occasions to indulge in the spontaneous expression of emotion. On other occasions, however, it can be positively harmful.

Recent evidence has pointed to the possible dangers of talking about one's emotions at the wrong time. The evidence concerns a kind of psychological therapy known as 'debriefing'. Debriefing is given to victims of traumatic events in many Western countries. As soon as there is a major disaster, such as a rail crash or a hijacking, counsellors are flown out to the scene along with the emergency services. After being treated by doctors for physical injury, the victims are treated by the counsellors for 'psychological injury'. The treatment involves going over the memories of the traumatic event and talking through all the feelings they inspire.

Debriefing differs in many ways from classical Freudian psychoanalysis, but it is based on the same underlying idea—namely, the idea that talking about the negative emotions should allow them to dissipate harmlessly. If this were true, those who undergo debriefing immediately after a traumatic event should suffer fewer long-term symptoms than those who don't. According to psychologist Jo Rick, however, things are the other way round: debriefing actually makes things worse. In one study of road-accident victims, she found that those who had undergone debriefing had more flashbacks and more fear a year after the accident than those who had not.

In the light of the past few decades of brain research, it is now easy to see why talking about traumatic memories is likely to make things worse rather than better. When left unexamined, bad memories do not fester like some untreated wound, as Freud thought. Rather, they tend to fade away via a process known as 'extinction'. By contrast, if the neural circuits encoding memories are continually reactivated by recounting the original experiences, extinction is prevented. Talking about old memories does not help them to go away. On the contrary, it keeps them alive, as Adam Smith recognized long before neuroscientists discovered the process of extinction. In *The Theory of Moral Sentiments*, he noted that, 'by relating their misfortunes', those who seek sympathy 'awaken in their memory the remembrance of those circumstances that occasioned their affliction. Their tears accordingly flow faster than before, and they are apt to abandon themselves to all the weakness of sorrow.'

The sensory route to happiness

In addition to language, humans have discovered many other technologies of mood in their quest to find short cuts to happiness. The use of colour is a case in point. For thousands of years, humans have decorated their own bodies and their surroundings with unusually bright colours that stimulate our visual systems much as chocolate stimulates our taste buds. Ever since the discovery of the first artificial dyes, such as the red ochre with which our ancestors painted their bodies around 100,000 years ago, we have used bright colours for their emotional effects.

Colour rarely affects our emotions directly. In some mental disorders such as autism the sight of a particularly bright colour may be enough to trigger a wave of panic, but in most people colour influences emotion indirectly via its influence on mood. Being in a red room may not itself make us angry, but it may gradually put us into an irritable mood in which we are more prone to lose our temper. The Italian film director Michelangelo Antonioni once painted the canteen red to put his actors in the mood for some tense scenes, but after a few weeks he noticed that other workers using the canteen had become more aggressive and had even come to blows.

Some of the most convincing scientific evidence about the effects of colour on mood comes from some experiments conducted by the psychologist Nicholas Humphrey. Humphrey put monkeys into specially designed cages each consisting of two chambers connected by a tunnel. When one chamber was lit by a blue light and the other by a red light, the monkeys consistently preferred the blue one. They would venture into the red chamber out of curiosity, and then quickly retreat into the blue chamber, where they would remain. If both chambers were red, the monkeys ran back and forth from one chamber to the other, without settling in either. Red made the monkeys irritable and nervous, while blue put them in a relaxed mood.

Red and blue produce similar emotional effects in humans. When people are exposed to red light, blood pressure rises, breathing speeds up, and the heart beats faster. Subjectively, people feel warmer in red rooms but also more nervous and aggressive. Blue light has the opposite effects. These responses are not merely cultural artefacts; two-week-old babies can be soothed more easily in blue than in red light, which suggests that at least part of our emotional response to colour is innate. But why should natural selection have programmed our minds in this way? How could a taste for certain colours or an aversion to others possibly have helped our ancestors to survive? Does red owe its warming effect to the fact that the two sources of heat our ancestors had—sunlight and firelight—are both this colour? What about the anxiety-provoking character of red light then?

Whatever the reason for our innate colour preferences, nature rarely offers us the sight of a large expanse of a single colour. A vivid sunset may occasionally paint the whole sky in one consistent shade of pink or purple, but nature's beauties are more usually mosaics. A peacock's tail and a beautiful landscape both offer a myriad different shades to the viewer's eye, not a monochromatic expanse like Antonioni's red canteen. By taking a single colour out of its natural setting, and using it to fill the entire visual field, paint and lighting amplify the natural effects of colour. In the technical terms of biology, artificial colours are 'super-stimuli'. They achieve their effects by keying into the same evolved preferences that nature touches, but they strike the keys much more forcefully. Compared to the neon glow of rococo art, nature is 'too green and badly lit', remarked the painter François Boucher.

A single uniform patch of colour is not always more emotionally powerful than a mosaic, however. What the mosaic loses in simplicity it can gain from careful arrangement. The emotional effects of such arrangements vary much more from person to person than the effects of single colours, so that one painting may produce a profound effect on one person while leaving another person cold. However, there are still some remarkable regularities in our aesthetic preferences. When asked to choose between a selection of abstract paintings, most people prefer the same one. Furthermore, they usually prefer the one painted by a famous artist rather than versions of this that have been modified in random ways by a computer. The original paintings must embody features that the human visual system is programmed to find most appealing. At present, scientists do not know what these features are, but the artists who painted the popular paintings must have had some intuitive appreciation of them. As the landscape painter John Constable remarked, painting is a science of which pictures are but the experiments. Both abstract art and representational art require considerable skill on the part of the artist, even if this consists only in distinguishing the experiments that work from those that do not.

Just as various colours may be arranged to produce a pleasing image, so sounds of varying frequency may be arranged to produce a pleasing melody. Music, like visual art, is a technology designed to tap directly into our perceptual capacities purely for the sake of producing pleasure. In Steven Pinker's words, music is 'auditory cheesecake'; for Shakespeare, music was also the food of love, indicating that music can also fuel emotions other than joy.

Like visual art, music usually affects our emotions indirectly, by changing our mood. Supermarkets do not use soft music to make us happy directly; that would rather defeat their objective, since the supermarket bosses do not want you to feel fulfilled by the music itself. Rather, they hope that the music will put you in a relaxed mood, which will in turn make you more sensitive to happiness-inducing thoughts, such as the anticipated pleasure of consuming an expensive chocolate cake.

Many compositions by Mozart, such as *Eine kleine Nachtmusik*, reliably produce good moods in those who hear them. This happens even if the listener is not particularly keen on classical music, which suggests that good composers tap into universal musical preferences in the way that good artists tap into universal visual preferences. Neuroscientists have found that when a person listens to a classical melody, neurons in different brain regions fire more synchronously than when the person listens to a random sequence of the same notes. The reason for this sense of melody, however, is still a mystery.

In humans, as in other primates, the visual system is highly developed, followed closely by the auditory system. The other sensory modalities are much less complex, or at least we are much less aware of their complexity. So it is not surprising that the sensory technologies of mood we esteem the most—art and music—are those that gratify our eyes and ears, while those that appeal to our other senses are accorded less dignity. Nevertheless, the senses of smell, taste, and touch have not been neglected. The emotional effects of different smells are poorly understood, though aromatherapists have developed some interesting taxonomies. The perfume industry is based on the emotional power of smell, and in many religions, from Buddhism to Christianity, worshippers burn incense to put themselves in a more contemplative mood.

The emotional effect of touch is better understood. Being caressed by another person releases natural opiates in the brain that are associated with a relaxed frame of mind. The evolutionary basis for this may lie in our primate past, when humans shared a common ancestor with chimpanzees, some five million years ago. Grooming may well have been as important for these primates as it is for modern chimpanzees, who spend hours each day removing the ticks from each other's fur. This grooming does not merely rid the other chimp of parasites; it also serves as a reliable sign of friendship. A preference for such a reliable signal of friendship would have motivated our furry ancestors to seek out friends. Those who did not like being groomed would have found themselves without allies when it came to a fight.

Just as our evolved visual preferences are the raw material for visual art, so our evolved tactile preferences are the raw material for massage. Massage is an ancient technology, like art and music. It was practised by the ancient Egyptians, and Hippocrates recommended doctors to 'be experienced in many things but assuredly in rubbing'. Today, orthodox medicine is beginning to rediscover the therapeutic value of massage, while it has been one of the central aspects of many alternative therapies for decades.

Cooking can be seen as a gustatory technology of mood. By processing natural foods in a variety of ways, and combining them according to well-tested recipes, cooking does for natural flavours what painting does for natural colours and music for natural sounds. It cranks them up into super-stimuli, tickling our taste buds more seductively than nature ever did. If strawberries taste good because they are sweet, cooks can make even sweeter things that taste twice as good like strawberry ice cream. Here, natural selection takes her revenge on us for daring to take the short cut to happiness instead of following the winding paths she set up for us to follow. Having given us a cheap and simple mechanism for finding glucose—a sweet tooth—she left us open to the dangers of wanting more than is good for us. In the stone age, that did not matter, since sugar came mostly in relatively diluted forms like fruit (honey being a notable exception). Today, however, where sugar comes in concentrated lumps called sweets and candies, our intense desire for it can pose a serious problem for health. Obesity is now reaching epidemic levels in many affluent countries and this is due largely to the dangerous combination of evolved desires for large amounts of sugar and fat, and the novel technology that is cooking.

Gustatory technologies of mood aim to induce good moods by stimulating our taste buds or by producing other chemical effects further downstream in the digestive process. Chocolate is quite an effective mood booster, as indeed are most foods and drinks that contain sugar. However, research has shown that, while most people feel more positive and energetic immediately after eating a chocolate bar, this effect soon wanes, and an hour afterwards they tend to feel even worse than they did before eating the chocolate in the first place. Tea and coffee have similar effects, with a short-term boost in mood being followed by a medium-term decrease. Most drugs have the same effect. In fact, the distinction between food and drugs is a rather arbitrary one, and even today there is still no scientific basis for distinguishing drugs from the various other kinds of substance we consume. We tend to call something a drug if we consume it primarily for its psychotropic effects rather than for its nutritional or gustatory ones, but most kinds of food and drink have some effect on your state of mind. Cottage cheese and chicken liver, for example, both contain high levels of tryptophan, which the brain uses to make a chemical called serotonin, which in turn is associated with good moods. Drugs are best seen as the end of a continuum of foods rather than a completely separate category.

Better living through chemistry

Drugs are perhaps the most direct short cut to happiness. For those suffering from a severe case of depression, the chemical route to happiness may be the only one. Even so, many people feel reluctant to ask their doctor for antidepressants, even when nothing else seems to work for them. The same people might have no qualms about drinking a glass of wine, but when it comes to using mood-altering drugs for therapeutic purposes there is a curious aversion. Depression, they feel, is something that one must overcome on one's own. Using drugs to deal with it betrays some kind of moral weakness. The psychiatrist Gerald Klerman coined the term 'pharmacological Calvinism' to refer to this perverse attitude to antidepressants.

Whether mood-altering drugs are used for therapeutic purposes, as when a depressed patient is prescribed Prozac, or for recreational purposes, as when a partygoer takes Ecstasy, the chemical action is similar. Both Prozac and Ecstasy boost levels of serotonin. This has led some people to propose that serotonin is the chemical basis of happiness. According to this theory, when there are high levels of serotonin in the brain, we are in a good mood, and when serotonin levels fall we get depressed. However, the evidence for this theory is mixed. Despite some claims that serotonin levels are depleted in the brains of suicidal patients, no abnormalities in the serotonin system have been consistently found in depressed people. Also, antidepressant drugs like Prozac boost serotonin levels in the brain as quickly as recreational drugs like Ecstasy—typically within an hour or two, while depressed patients have to take daily doses of Prozac for two or three weeks before they experience any alleviation of their symptoms. So moods cannot be just a question of serotonin levels in the brain. At present, despite the claims of various pharmaceutical companies, which have found that the seductive simplicity of the serotonin hypothesis makes it ideal for marketing their products, our understanding of how antidepressant drugs work is still in its infancy.

Other brain chemicals besides serotonin, such as dopamine and noradrenaline, also play an important part in mood. Drugs that affect these chemicals can also be used to change one's emotional state. Cocaine and amphetamines boost levels of dopamine and noradrenaline in the brain, and this is what seems to give them their euphoric properties. However, other drugs such as chlorpromazine, which boost levels of these chemicals almost as quickly as cocaine or amphetamine, do not produce the same instant euphoria, so once again the neural basis of mood must be more complicated than merely how much dopamine or noradrenaline you have sloshing around in your brain.

As with chocolate, tea, and sugar, the mood-enhancing effects of most recreational drugs are short term, and the high may be followed by a distinctly unpleasant comedown. It is possible to maintain the high by taking another dose before the effects of the first wear off, but, the longer you stay up, the worse the eventual comedown. In an attempt to postpone the comedown indefinitely, some people become addicts, taking the drug continuously to maintain a permanent high. In such cases, maintaining the drug habit becomes the only valued activity in life, as everything else fades into insignificance. In an experiment conducted by James Olds, a rat was placed in a cage with a lever attached to a wire by means of which a current was applied to an electrode implanted in the reward centre of its brain. Every time the rat pressed the lever, the electrode stimulated a little burst of dopamine similar to the rush produced by cocaine. It was not long before the rat was spending all its time pressing the lever repeatedly, ignoring everything else around it, even food—a perfect image of the drug addict.

As the addict's body and brain adapt to the drug, ever larger doses become necessary to achieve the same high. The long-term effects of pumping so much of the drug into the body are usually severe damage to various organs. Prolonged regular snorting of cocaine usually leads to sinusitis, nosebleeds, and a perforated nasal septum, and eventually heart attacks, strokes, and psychosis. Alcohol, one of the most addictive drugs, affects nearly every organ system, so alcoholics have increased rates of liver cirrhosis, stomach cancer, heart disease, and amnesia. With smoking, it is not the nicotine that poisons the body so much as the other components of the cigarette—tar and nitrogen dioxide—which cause heart disease, and lung cancer.

Most drug-users manage to avoid these dangers by keeping their habit under control. Just as the majority of those who drink alcohol do not become alcoholics, so there are many people who use marijuana, Ecstasy, and cocaine without ever becoming addicted. Any drug, from tobacco and tea to cocaine and heroin, can be used responsibly if proper care is taken. Many respectable people used cocaine in the late 19th century, especially in the impure form that was an ingredient in the original Coca-Cola. Victorian gentlemen could often be seen smoking opium in the various dens around London. Sherlock Holmes injected morphine. The hysteria surrounding the use of such drugs today is a product of the current regulatory regime.

No drug is without side effects. Even the most recent designer drugs have effects other than those for which they are prescribed. Besides alleviating depression, Prozac can increase anxiety, at least during the first few weeks of treatment. More subtle side effects of Prozac that have been reported include a sense of emotional numbness or distance, and lower sensitivity to the emotional needs of others. So, as a short cut to happiness, drugs are double-edged swords. Used wisely and responsibly, they can certainly brighten up one's life on occasion. On the other hand, the dangers of addiction threaten the unwary.

Film and emotion

In choosing our short cuts to happiness, we are not necessarily faced with a stark alternative between the various technologies of mood. We can pick and mix, combining them in accordance with our tastes and values. The mixing of different art forms was held in high esteem by the Romantics, who coined the term 'synaesthesia' for such combinations. The prime example was opera, which combines drama, poetry, music, song, dance, and painting to produce a cornucopia of sensory delights. Films, musicals, and video games can be seen as modern forms of synaesthesia.

The cinema is a particularly powerful technology of mood, yet until recently film theory did not pay much attention to the emotions. This is now changing, and researchers from a wide variety of disciplines are beginning to study the ways that films evoke emotional experiences in the viewer. Neuroscientists are using functional magnetic resonance imaging (fMRI) to explore the ways that the brain responds to films, but in these experiments the viewer must lie down inside an unfamiliar machine. Other researchers attempt to capture audience responses in more realistic settings by using an infrared camera to detect the moments when viewers blink. Using these and other methods, scientists hope to understand how the technical details of moviemaking, such as frame rates and scene structure, affect perceptual and cognitive processing.

As we learn more about what makes films engaging, this research might help studios to make better movies. Yet this may not be entirely beneficial. Besides being sources of fun and pleasure, movies can also convey powerful ideological messages, sometimes in ways that viewers may be unaware of. The political slant of the propaganda films made by Leni Riefenstahl may be obvious, but other movies may be more subtle and therefore more effective.

If psychologists can help film directors make better movies, then it is also true that film directors can help psychologists understand more about emotions. As the psychologist Jeffrey Zacks says, we have now accumulated over a hundred years of experiments in moviemaking. These contain many lessons about perception, memory, and emotion which psychologists have barely begun to explore.

Chapter 4
The head and the heart

Emotions are fairly transient states. For much of the time, we are not in the grip of fear, nor swooning with love. In this neutral frame of mind, we can often think quite rationally. We are clear-headed and can spot bad arguments quite easily. Things are quite different, however, when a strong emotion wells up in us, or a powerful mood takes us over. At these times the head becomes a slave to the heart.

People have long been interested in the way that emotions affect our cognitive capacities. In his book on rhetoric, Aristotle noted that 'feelings are conditions that cause us to change and alter our judgements'. In recent years, a growing amount of experimental work has helped to pinpoint the nature of these effects. This chapter explores some of this work in relation to three cognitive capacities: attention, memory, and logical reasoning.

The mental spotlight

Attention is the name that psychologists give to our capacity to focus on a particular thought or activity. It is like a spotlight that can be pointed at different mental activities. Even though there might be hundreds of things going on in our minds, we can train our mental spotlight on only one of them at a time. When we are concentrating hard on something like a crossword puzzle or a difficult sum, other thoughts fade away. Emotions can interrupt our thoughts and redirect our attention elsewhere. The sound of an explosion triggers a burst of fear, which makes us forget what we were doing before and focus on the source of the danger.

Spotlights can be more or less focused. When focused to their maximum extent, they illuminate a very small area with a very bright light. When de-focused, they illuminate a larger area, but the light is less intense. The same is true for attention. When we are relaxed, and not in the grip of any particular emotion, our mental spotlight is relatively unfocused, and more thoughts may drift through our awareness. When an emotion occurs, however, our mental spotlight suddenly contracts, focusing on one small thought to the exclusion of all others. This thought is usually a representation of the external object that caused the emotion. When we are afraid, for example, the mental spotlight focuses on the thing that frightened us. Anger makes us dwell on the thing that annoyed us. Love makes it hard to think of anything except the beloved. Emotions are often blamed for distracting us, so it might seem strange to say that they help to focus our attention. There is, however, no contradiction; emotions distract us from one thought only in order to make us pay attention to another.

Attention is affected by moods too. Moods, you will recall, are different from emotions. They typically last much longer than basic emotions, working in the background by raising or lowering our susceptibility to emotional stimuli. Like emotions, however, moods force the mental spotlight to contract, though probably not as much as emotions do (happiness may be an exception to this rule, enlarging our attention, making the spotlight more diffuse). People in an anxious mood tend to be preoccupied by thoughts of their own safety, but, unlike someone in a state of fright, they are able to think about a few other things too.

Like emotions, moods tend to make us focus on thoughts about the things that caused the mood. When we are in an irritable mood, we may brood about someone who has recently annoyed us. Sometimes, however, a mood may overtake us without focusing our attention on anything in particular. We may become anxious without being aware of the cause of our anxiety. Such 'free-floating' anxiety still affects attention, however. Instead of forcing us to focus on a particular thought, it clears thoughts away, prompting us to attend to the world around us. If we walk down a dark alley late at night, an anxious mood leads us to scan the shadows for signs of movement. In this situation, anxiety is clearly a useful thing. A person in an anxious mood is on the lookout for threats and is therefore able to respond more quickly should anything untoward actually occur. The threats need not be physical. Anything that might prevent you from achieving a goal can be seen as a threat.

If, however, your goal is to give a good speech at your best friend's wedding, the biggest threat might be your tendency to stutter when nervous. An anxious mood would then prompt you to be on the lookout for the tiniest hint of hesitation in your speech. Should you notice such hesitation, of course, this will only make you more anxious, and you may find yourself degenerating into a nervous stammer. On such occasions, anxiety becomes counterproductive.

Psychologists have investigated the effects of anxiety on attention by means of an experiment known as the 'emotional Stroop test'. The original Stroop test has nothing to do with emotion. It involves showing people words printed in different colours and asking them to say what the colour was. The time between the moment when the word appears on the screen, and the moment when the person gives the right answer, is carefully measured. The trick is that some of the words are also the names of colours, and sometimes the colour of the ink in which these words are printed is different from the colour named by the word. When this happens, it is mildly confusing, so that reaction times are slower. People are quicker at saying what the colour of the ink is when it matches the colour named by the word—when the word 'red' is printed in red ink, for example—than when it does not.

The emotional version of the Stroop test uses words with strong emotional connotations rather than the names of colours, but, like the original Stroop test, the words are still printed in different coloured inks, and people are asked to say what the colour of the ink is. When people are shown a word with strong emotional connotations, they typically take longer to say what the colour of the ink is than when the word is emotionally neutral. Of course, different words carry different emotional connotations for different people. Words connected with rape, for example, will be more emotionally charged for rape victims than for others. This shows up in the emotional Stroop test too. One study found that, compared to other people, rape victims were much slower at saying what the colour of the ink was when the words were related to rape. It appears that the anxiety generated by seeing a word connected with a traumatic experience focuses the attention on the meaning of the word, making it harder to pay attention to peripheral details like the colour of the ink in which the word is printed.

Emotion and memory

Besides affecting attention, emotions and moods also play an important part in memory. When something is stored in the memory, it is not recorded in all its finest detail, but rather filed away under a few keywords. When we come to recall something from memory, we extract some of these keywords, and fill in the rest by educated guesswork. Remembering is, therefore, never exact. It is more like reconstructing an antique pot from a few broken shards than replaying an old movie. Some memories seem so fresh and vivid when we recall them that we may have the impression of reliving the event exactly as it happened, but this is an illusion caused by the power of our imaginative reconstruction. When we compare such recollections with those of others who were in the same place at the same time, we may find that the accounts differ markedly, while the differing versions seem equally vivid and real to each person.

The ease and accuracy with which we recall an event are affected by both the emotional state we were in when the event occurred and the mood we are in when we recall it. Freud thought that memories of negatively charged emotional events would be 'repressed' and therefore harder to recall, but in fact precisely the opposite is the case. Traumatic memories do not retreat into some dark recess of the mind, as Freud supposed. Rather, they obtrude persistently into consciousness, perturbing us when we would rather forget them, even disrupting our dreams. In severe cases, this is known as 'post-traumatic stress disorder', a syndrome characterized by vivid flashbacks in which the person relives the event in painful detail.

Emotions help to etch events more deeply in our memories. Any event that produces a strong emotion in us, whether negative or positive, is recalled more easily and more accurately than an emotionally neutral event. In one study, three groups of students were shown a set of fifteen slides, each of which showed a sight that you might see while walking to work. Each group saw the same set of slides, except for slide number eight, of which there were three different versions (see Figure 3).

In one version, a woman was riding a bicycle. In another, the same woman was carrying the bicycle on her shoulder. In the third version, the woman was lying by the roadside with the bicycle lying next to her, as if she had been knocked down by a car. When asked to recall what they had seen, the group who had been shown the slide with the woman lying on the ground remembered the colour of her coat much better than the other groups, but they were much worse at recalling peripheral details such as the colour of a car in the distance. This suggests that the core features of emotionally charged events are remembered better than those of neutral events; the peripheral features, however, fade away more quickly.

3. The three versions of the critical eighth slide in the sequence
used by Christianson and Loftus.

The ease and accuracy of recall are also influenced by the mood we are in when we remember something. Dozens of experiments conducted by the psychologist Gordon Bower show that, when we are in a happy mood, we tend to recall pleasant events more easily and more accurately than unpleasant ones. The opposite is true when we are in a sad mood. This phenomenon is known as 'mood-congruent recall'. In one experiment, Bower asked people to recall incidents of any kind from their childhood, and to describe each one. The next day, when the same people were in a neutral mood, he asked them to label each incident as pleasant, unpleasant, or neutral. The following day, a happy or a sad mood was artificially induced in each person by means of hypnotic suggestion, and they were then asked to recall as many of the incidents as they could. Bower found that those in a good mood remembered many of the incidents they had labelled as pleasant, but few of those they had labelled as unpleasant. Those in a bad mood, on the other hand, remembered more of the unpleasant incidents.

A possible explanation for the phenomenon of mood-congruent recall is that, when events are stored in the memory, they are tagged with an emotional marker indicating which emotion, if any, was present when the event was experienced. When we recall events from memory, those that are tagged with a marker that is compatible with the current emotional state are given more salience. Keith Oatley and Jennifer Jenkins have suggested that this may help us to deal with a current situation more easily by bringing to mind incidents comparable to the one that provoked the current mood.

Judging people and evaluating arguments

In addition to their effects on attention and memory, emotions and moods also exert a powerful influence on decision-making and judgement. For example, the opinions we form of other people are often affected by the mood we happen to be in when we meet them. People in a good mood are likely to judge the same person more positively than people in a bad mood. In one experiment, good and bad moods were induced artificially by telling people that they had done very well or very badly in a mock test. They were then asked to interview someone by asking them a prearranged set of questions, such as 'What are your most important traits'. What the students didn't know was that the people they were interviewing were in league with the experimenters, and all gave exactly the same answers to the questions. The answers were deliberately ambiguous, revealing both positive things ('I'm pretty friendly') and negative things ('I'm quite stubborn and impatient') about the interviewee. Afterwards, the interviewers were asked to evaluate the interviewee on personal and professional grounds. Sure enough, the interviewers who had been put in a good mood tended to rate the interviewees more positively than those who had been put in a bad mood, even though the answers they received were the same. Those in a good mood were also more likely to say that they would hire the interviewee for a job.

It is not just happy and sad moods that influence our judgements of other people. Anxiety can also affect the way we see others. The precise way in which it affects such judgements, however, is quite surprising. Rather than making us view strangers in a negative way, being in an anxious mood can actually make us feel closer to them. This, at least, seems to be the conclusion of one famous experiment conducted in the 1970s. Men crossing a high, rather scary suspension bridge were stopped by a young woman, who asked them if they would take part in a survey. She then gave them a card with her phone number on, saying that she would be happy to talk to them about the survey in greater detail if they wanted. Later the same day, she did the same thing on a much lower and safer bridge. During the following days, many more phone calls were received from the men who had met the woman on the scary bridge than from those who had met her on the safe one. The anxiety seems to have made them more friendly, perhaps even flirtatious.

This bonding effect of anxiety may provide part of the explanation for the strange phenomenon of hostages coming to care deeply about their captors. Some of this may simply be due to the close proximity in which hostages and captors live during their brief relationships, but even so it seems possible that the affection for one's captor is intensified by the anxiety that lurks constantly in the mind of the hostage. This conjunction of anxiety and affection seems counter-intuitive, but there may be an evolutionary reason for it. Perhaps it evolved to help our ancestors join forces in dangerous situations, when there was safety in numbers.

As well as affecting the way we judge other people, moods also influence our susceptibility to weak arguments. Here, though, it is not just a question of what mood one happens to be in when listening to the argument, but also of how much time one has to think about it. When people are in a neutral mood, or have lots of time to think, bad arguments are not very persuasive. But when they are in a good mood and have little time to think, people are more influenced by invalid arguments (and less by valid ones). It seems that the combination of being in a good mood and being in a rush forces one to take short cuts, basing one's judgement less on logical analysis and more on contextual clues such as the reputation of the speaker.

To test this idea, Diane Mackie and Leila Worth quizzed American students to see whether or not they were in favour of greater gun control. A positive mood was then induced in half of the students by showing them a five-minute extract from a comedy programme. The others watched an emotionally neutral extract from a programme about wine. Each group was then presented with an argument advancing a view about gun control that ran contrary to their own opinions. Those who were in favour of greater gun control read an argument opposing such restrictions, while those against gun control read an argument in favour. Half were presented with weak arguments and half with strong logical arguments. Some of the students were told that the person presenting the argument was an expert, while others were told that they were reading the views of a first-year student. Furthermore, some were given a short time to read the argument, while others were allowed to take as long as they wanted. After reading the argument, the students were re-tested to see if their views on gun control had changed.

Overall, everyone was more influenced by the good arguments than by the bad ones (see Figure 4). But, for those in a positive mood with little time to think, the difference was very small. Whereas all the other groups found the weak arguments much less persuasive, those in a good mood and in a rush found the bad arguments almost as persuasive as the good ones. Further testing revealed that this group had given much more weight to the reputation of the speaker when reading the argument. The fact that the happy people who were allowed to take as long as they

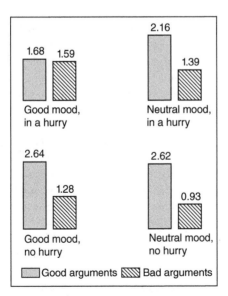

4. **Graph of results from Mackie and Worth experiment.**

wanted found the weak arguments as unpersuasive as those in a bad mood might seem to point to time being the crucial variable rather than mood. However, when Mackie and Worth compared the actual time taken by the two groups who were allowed to examine the arguments as long as they wanted, they found that those in a good mood actually took longer than those in a bad mood. They concluded from this that being in a good mood makes you more easily swayed by bad arguments, but that most people seem to be aware of this fact at some level, and so automatically compensate for this by taking longer to think about things when their critical powers are blunted by happiness.

The research of Mackie and Worth suggests that there are two ways of forming judgements about complex issues. One way is slow but very precise. The other is quick and dirty. The slow but precise way relies mainly on logic, but the quick and dirty way relies heavily on emotion. Reason and emotion can thus be seen as two complementary systems in the human brain for making decisions. When it is important to get the answer right, and we have a lot of time and information at our disposal, we can use the slow and clean method of reasoning things through. When we have little time and information, or it is not so important to get the right answer, we can switch to the fast and frugal method of following our feelings.

Sometimes, however, we use the wrong system. For example, we may overestimate the amount of time and information we have at our disposal or the importance of getting the decision right, and then end up reasoning about something when we would have been better off consulting our feelings. The neuroscientist Antonio Damasio tells a story about a brain-damaged patient of his who could not help overusing the rational system. After a check-up, Damasio asked the patient when he would like to come for his next appointment. When Damasio suggested two possible dates, just a few days apart, the patient pulled out his diary and began to list the advantages and disadvantages of attending on each.

For almost half an hour, he weighed up the possible weather conditions on each day, the need to cancel other engagements, and dozens of other relevant factors. Damasio listened to all this with great patience, before finally suggesting, quietly, that the patient should come on the second of the two dates. 'OK', smiled the patient, snapping shut his diary as if nothing odd had happened.

As this story illustrates, when there is not much at stake in making a decision, we are better off saving time by using the quick and dirty emotional system rather than the slower rational one. On the other hand, there are times when it is so important to arrive at the right judgement that considerations of time are better left aside. For example, when we want to find out whether or not someone is guilty of murder, getting the answer right is so important that we are prepared to sacrifice time for accuracy. In such cases, the impact of emotions on decision-making can be positively harmful, and we seek ways of diminishing their influence.

It is widely supposed that one way to do this is to institutionalize the decision-making process, transforming it from an individual action into a collective one. The hope is that, in the communal debate, the emotional biases of individuals will cancel each other out, leaving pure reason to emerge as the exclusive basis for judgement. Two heads are supposed to be better than one, because they are supposed to be less emotional. In science, the peer review process is supposed to filter out the rival emotions of various disputants, so that they may reach agreement by purely rational means. In the legal system of most countries today, decisions about important cases are taken not by a single judge but by a jury of twelve. Once again, the hope is that twelve heads will be better than one, because their conflicting emotions will cancel each other out, leaving pure reason to be the final arbiter.

Unfortunately, there are reasons to doubt this rosy view of institutional decision-making. Being in a group may amplify emotions rather than tempering them. Writing at the end of the 19th century, the French psychologist Gustave LeBon described in chilling terms how people can be swept away by the passions of the crowd, working themselves up into a frenzy more vicious than anything of which they would be capable on their own. More recently, psychologists have speculated that demagogues such as Hitler and Mussolini achieved and maintained their power in part by taking advantage of a primitive 'group mind', in which collective emotion drowns out the individual voice of reason.

Other research paints a more positive picture of group decision-making. James Surowiecki has marshalled evidence showing that, under certain circumstances, groups can make decisions that are better than could have been made by any single member of the group. However, this tends to be the case only when there is a diversity of opinion and when people make their judgements independently before pooling them. In other words, too much communication can make the group as a whole less intelligent. Emotional contagion can be seen as a kind of nonverbal communication which exacerbates the problem.

For good or ill, and perhaps both, the tendency for emotion to be amplified in social groups begs for explanation. Are we programmed to be conformists, secretly fascinated by the power of authority, as the psychologists of the Frankfurt School wondered darkly in the aftermath of the Second World War? Or is there a deeper biological reason for the power of emotional contagion?

The neural basis of empathy

The discovery of mirror neurons provides intriguing clues about the neural mechanisms involved in emotional contagion. Mirror neurons are activated in the same way regardless of whether an animal performs a given action or whether the animal observes the same action performed by another. In the 1980s and 1990s, neurophysiologists at the University of Parma placed electrodes in the brains of macaque monkeys to study neurons specialized in the control of hand and mouth actions. During each experiment, the researchers allowed the monkey to reach for pieces of food and measured the response to certain movements. They found that some neurons responded both when the monkey observed a person picking up a piece of food, and also when the monkey itself picked up the food.

It is not ethical to do the same experiments with humans, so the evidence for mirror neurons in humans is indirect. This evidence is derived mainly from functional magnetic resonance imaging (fMRI) studies, For example, one study found that the same brain regions were activated when people smelled disgusting odours and when they saw expressions of disgust on the faces of other people inhaling the same odours. Mirror neurons may therefore act like a kind of reflex mechanism: first you see an expression of disgust on someone else's face, and this automatically triggers feelings of disgust in you yourself (see Box 6). This is what I mean by emotional contagion.

The capacity for emotional contagion may be a crucial foundation for empathy, but it is not the whole story. Empathy means feeling someone else's emotions as if they were your own. For example, if a close friend breaks out in tears over some personal misfortune, we may feel overwhelmed by sadness too and shed tears of our own. This is similar to emotional contagion, and involves some of the same neural circuits, but it is not merely an automatic, reflex response, for it also involves some higher cognitive processing, and this may modulate the degree to which we share the other person's feelings.

For example, in one study participants were asked to play a game in which the other player (who was secretly in league with the experimenter) could follow either a fair or an unfair strategy. Next, the participants watched as the other player seemed to

Box 6 Subliminal reactions to emotional faces

In 1998, the Irish neuroscientist Ray Dolan, together with colleagues John Morris and Arne Öhman, found that the brain processes facial expressions of emotion at an unconscious as well as at a conscious level. In one experiment, they showed two slides of angry faces to people. While one of the slides was shown, a burst of unpleasant 'white noise' was played, thus ensuring that the memory of this face would have a negative affective marker attached to it. The other angry face was presented without any accompanying sound.

In the next part of the experiment, one of the slides was flashed up very quickly, immediately followed by a slide of an expressionless face. This is called 'backward masking', because perception of the second slide masks the perception of the first. When asked what they saw, subjects reported seeing the second slide, but not the first.

Even though they did not report seeing the first slide, the subjects must have perceived it at some unconscious level, because their brain activity was different depending on whether the first slide was the one that was associated with the unpleasant noise or not. In other words, the first slide had been perceived subliminally. The main brain region associated with the unconscious recognition of the negatively charged face was the right amygdala. Once again, the amygdala had turned out to play a crucial role in unconscious emotional processing. Whenever you have a gut reaction to someone you have never met—whenever, that is, you 'just don't like the look of someone'—it is probably because your amygdala is telling you that the stranger looks like someone who has done something bad to you, even though you don't have any conscious recall of the old foe.

undergo painful electric shocks. Those whose partners had played fairly showed the normal brain responses found in other experiments that have studied how people respond to signs of pain in others. The brain responses in male participants were reduced, however, when they observed signs of pain in those who had played unfairly. Moreover, males but not females showed increased activation in brains areas associated with the desire for revenge.

These and similar findings indicate that empathy involves thoughts as well as feelings. We may well cry in sympathy with a close friend who breaks down in tears over the death of his mother, but the sight of a stranger in tears may leave us cold. If we see someone we actively dislike in tears, we may even experience Schadenfreude—joy in another's pain. All this suggests that it may be possible to train yourself to be more empathic by learning to redirect and refocus your thoughts. When you see a homeless person begging on the streets, for example, you might be tempted to write him off as an alcoholic. This is a convenient excuse for ignoring their plight. But what if you try to put yourself in their shoes? What if you try to think of ways that this person is like you—a person who feels lonely, who's probably experienced some kind of misfortune along the way, and who still has hopes and dreams? We can't all be saints, but we can all learn to be more compassionate and forgiving.

There are significant individual differences in the capacity for empathy. At one extreme, psychopaths (or sociopaths) seem to lack empathy altogether, which may go a long way to explain their tendencies to violence, deceit, and cunning. At the other end of the spectrum, some people seem to suffer from an excess of empathy; they are hypersensitive to other peoples' emotions. Highly empathic people may feel driven to fix everyone's problems and make them feel better This can be very stressful and lead to feelings of depression or burnout.

Cultivating the right amount of empathy is a key part of our ethical lives. Empathy leads to toleration, and this is crucial for building a more peaceful and interconnected world. The philosophers of the Enlightenment regarded fellow-feeling and sympathy as the fundamental building blocks of a healthy global society. This idea is more important now than ever.

At the time of writing, at the end of the second decade of the 21st century, intolerance and prejudice are on the rise. Nationalism and racism, which seemed to be in retreat in the decades following the Second World War, are once again gaining ground. Politicians talk about building walls to stop the flow of immigrants, and turn a blind eye to the suffering of refugees and asylum seekers. The world is badly in need of more empathy. Empathy makes us mindful of our commonality and connection with fellow humans the world over. It helps us look beneath the superficial differences of religion, race, or ideology, and see the underlying human nature that we all share.

Chapter 5
The computer that cried

Some of the most exciting research in emotion is now conducted not by psychologists or anthropologists, but by computer scientists. The new field of affective computing (sometimes called artificial emotional intelligence, or emotion AI) attempts to build systems and devices that can recognize and simulate human emotions. Some researchers even predict that machines will one day come to have emotions of their own.

Start with emotion recognition. The first serious attempts to give computers the ability to recognize human emotions began in the 1990s. Pioneering work was done by Ifran Essa and Alex Pentland, who programmed a computer to recognize facial expressions of six basic emotions. When volunteers made one of these expressions, the computer recognized the corresponding emotion correctly 98 per cent of the time. This was even better than the accuracy rate achieved by most humans on the same task.

A great deal of progress has been made since then. In addition to visual image processing, computers can also extract emotional information from other kinds of input such as audio and physiological data. Humans express emotions in a variety of ways, including tone of voice and subtle cues such as sweating and heart rate, so when computers have access to sensors that can detect this information, such as microphones and heart rate monitors, they can combine all the data from these various inputs to build up a more complex picture of a person's emotional state.

The emotional state can be described in one of two ways: as a discrete category, or as a point on a graph. The first approach involves mapping the input onto a specific category or label such as anger or fear. The second approach maps the input onto a point in a Cartesian coordinate system with two or more dimensions. Which approach one adopts depends on one's underlying theory of how best to classify emotions. Categorical approaches view emotions as distinct psychological states. Ekman's theory of basic emotions is a case in point; there is a list of emotions, and the computer must decide which of these best fits the input. Dimensional approaches see emotions more as a question of degree. For example, the Positive Activation–Negative Activation (PANA) model treats positive affect and negative affect as two separate dimensions along which emotions vary continuously. This can be represented as a two-dimensional graph in which the vertical axis represents positive affect and the horizontal axis represents negative affect. Alternatively, Hugo Lövheim has proposed a three-dimensional model in which each axis corresponds to levels of the neurotransmitters dopamine, noradrenaline, and serotonin. In the so-called Lövheim cube of emotion, the eight corners of the cube correspond to eight different emotions. For example, anger is defined as a combination of low serotonin, high dopamine, and high noradrenaline (see Figure 5). Whichever way a researcher chooses to classify emotions—whether categorical or dimensional—emotion recognition in computers is usually achieved by taking the input from the various sensors and using machine learning to map the input onto the relevant category or point.

Computers that can recognize and identify human emotions in this way can be used for a wide variety of purposes. For example, virtual assistants such as Apple's Siri, Google Assistant, and

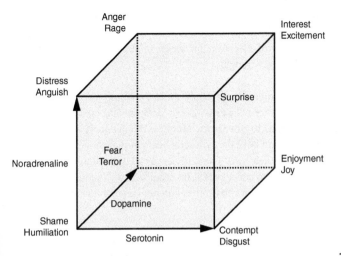

5. The Lövheim cube of emotion.

Amazon Alexa can understand the words we speak, but they often lack an ability to tell how annoyed or happy or depressed we are. A variety of companies are now working to remedy this. If a virtual assistant in an intelligent vehicle could recognize the emotional state of the driver, it might notice that she looks tired and offer to take the wheel. Your bathroom mirror might detect that you're feeling stressed and adjust the lighting while playing a soothing piece of music. An online learning environment could sense when a student is frustrated and slow down or tell a joke. Autistic people might use machines that can recognize emotional expressions to navigate social situations more effectively.

This technology carries risks as well as benefits. Employers might decide to scan workers' faces for signs of boredom. Facial recognition software might be used in job interviews to select the most enthusiastic candidates. If the algorithms are trained on data sets of mostly white faces, these systems may be biased against those from different ethnic groups. If the technology becomes prevalent in everyday life, it could even affect our intimate relationships. If husbands and wives can use their phones to spot subtle cues of deception, marriages might become more truthful but also more fraught.

There are more playful applications for emotion recognition technology too. The artist David McGoran has made a synthetic heart linked to a heartrate monitor. When people wear the monitor and hold the synthetic heart in their hands, it beats in time with their own. The experience can be profoundly moving. Together with colleagues at his studio, Rusty Squid, McGoran uses robotic technology to produce interactive artworks that inspire wonder and joy.

Affective computing is not limited to building systems that can recognize human emotions; it also involves building devices that can simulate emotional expressions. One early example is Kismet, a robotic head built by Cynthia Breazeal at MIT in the late 1990s. Kismet has movable eyelids, eyes, and lips (see Figure 6). The range of emotional expressions available to Kismet is limited, but they are convincing enough to generate feelings of sympathy among the humans who interact with it. Breazeal invited human parents to play with Kismet on a daily basis. When left alone, Kismet looked sad, but when it detected a human face, it smiled, inviting attention. If the human moved too fast, a look of fear warned that something was wrong. Human parents who played with Kismet couldn't help but respond sympathetically to these simple forms of emotional expression.

Kismet was designed in deliberately cartoon-like way. It had big eyes, furry eyebrows, and rubbery red lips. In other words, it was not designed to look human. When designers attempt to make robots look more human, they often run into what has been called 'the uncanny valley'. This phenomenon was first identified by the Japanese roboticist Masahiro Mori. Mori argued that, as the appearance of a robot is made more humanlike, people will react

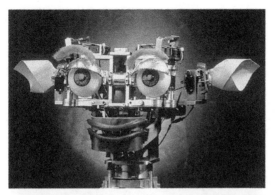

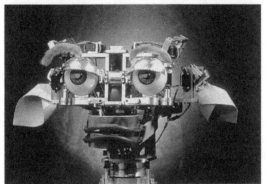

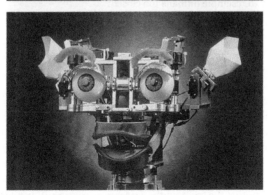

6. Kismet, robot developed at MIT, which imitates a range of
'human' emotions. Here happiness, sadness, and surprise.

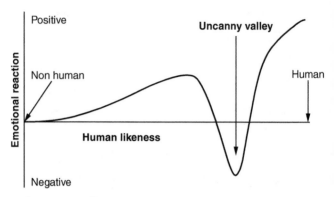

7. **The uncanny valley.**

in increasingly positive and empathetic ways until the robot reaches a point where the resemblance is almost perfect, but not complete. At that point, people suddenly find the robot disturbing (see Figure 7).

When designing emotional robots, therefore, engineers must also take care to investigate how people respond to their creations. It is not necessarily a good idea to aim for ever greater realism. On the contrary, people may be happier interacting with robots that do not try to resemble humans too closely.

Humans do not just express emotions by means of facial expression. The way we speak also reveals a lot about our emotional state. Kismet mimicked this by making cute little sounds like a baby. Computer scientists are building more sophisticated speech synthesizers that sound emotional by modulating non-linguistic aspects of vocalization such as speed, pitch, and volume. In one pioneering experiment, Janet Cahn fed a computer emotionally neutral sentences such as 'I saw your name in the paper', and then instructed it to say the sentence in a way that sounded sad. When human listeners were asked to say what emotion the voice synthesizer was expressing, 91 per cent of them guessed right. The program was not so good at expressing other emotions, but humans are not always successful in conveying their emotions by vocal signals alone either.

Affective computing has made great strides since the pioneering work of Cynthia Breazeal and Janet Cahn. A whole range of emotionally expressive robots now exist. Like Kismet, these robots are usually programmed to exhibit a fixed range of emotional expressions. The programmers start by identifying a list of emotions that they want the robot to simulate. In other words, they usually adopt a categorical approach to the classification of emotion. The engineers then devise distinct expressions for each emotion.

Machines that can simulate the expression of emotions can be used for a variety of purposes. They may, for example, to be used to help children with autism. LuxAI, a company spun out of the University of Luxembourg, has built a robot that they say can increase the willingness of autistic children to interact with human therapists, and decrease discomfort during therapy sessions. 'When you are interacting with a person, there are a lot of social cues such as facial expressions, tonality of the voice, and movement of the body which are overwhelming and distracting for children with autism,' says Aida Nazarikhorram, cofounder of LuxAI. 'But robots have this ability to make everything simplified. For example, every time the robot says something or performs a task, it's exactly the same as the previous time, and that gives comfort to children with autism.'

Emotionally expressive robots might also serve as artificial companions for elderly people. Gerontologists have known for some time that pets, especially animals like cats and dogs that exhibit a range of emotions, help prevent depression in the elderly. Similarly beneficial effects may be produced by electronic pets such as Sony's Aibo robot dog. Researchers are now building humanoid robots that may be even more rewarding companions.

As humanoid robots become ever more advanced, some have speculated that relationships with robot companions might one day be even more satisfying than relationships with humans. In his book *Love and Sex with Robots*, the British scholar David Levy argues that this will be commonplace by the middle of the 21st century. He predicts that many people will even marry robots and have sex with them. 'Love with robots will be as normal as love with other humans,' Levy writes, 'while the number of sexual acts and lovemaking positions commonly practiced between humans will be extended, as robots teach us more than is in all of the world's published sex manuals combined.'

Not everyone agrees. A loving relationship often involves the belief that you have been freely chosen by your partner and that they might therefore reject you. Although people typically want commitment and fidelity from their partners, they want these things to be the fruit of an ongoing choice, rather than inflexible behaviour patterns. It is doubtful that robots will be able to provide this.

Some go further and argue that sex robots are positively harmful. Kathleen Richardson warns that the development of sex robots will hinder the development of empathic relationships between humans and reinforce power relations of inequality and violence. Richardson founded the Campaign Against Sex Robots to combat the normalization of the idea that women could be replaced by sex machines as intimate others.

In a similar vein, Joanna Bryson has argued that robots should be built, marketed, and considered legally as slaves, not companion peers. In humanizing them, she claims, we dehumanize real people. Bryson argues that robots should not be described as persons, nor given legal nor moral responsibility for their actions. On the contrary, we should recognize that robots are our slaves. It is we who determine their goals and behaviour, either directly or indirectly through specifying their intelligence or how their intelligence is acquired. As we will see later, however, evolutionary approaches to designing robots may undermine such clear cut distinctions.

Emotions and action selection

The developments examined so far in this chapter all concern external aspects of emotion—facial expressions, tone of voice, and so on. When computer scientists program machines to recognize human expressions of emotion, or to simulate emotional expressions of their own, they are not attempting to give the machines internal states like ours. But there are computer scientists who attempt to do just this.

Why would computer scientists want to build machines that have inner emotional states rather than just fancy faces? One reason involves something known as action selection. Action selection is a technical term for something that appears rather simple, but which is in fact very complex—the problem of deciding what to do next. Even the most basic of animals must choose from a range of possible actions available to them.

Take bees for example. Bees fly from flower to flower collecting nectar to carry back to the hive. After collecting nectar from one flower, a bee must decide whether to return to the hive or fly to another flower. If the bee visits another flower it might get more nectar, but the weight of the extra nectar will make it harder to fly. In fact, carrying too much nectar can shorten a bee's lifespan. The shorter the lifespan of a worker bee, the less overall time it has to contribute to its colony. A bee must somehow weigh up the costs and benefits of each action when deciding whether to continue collecting nectar or fly back home.

Robots face similar dilemmas. An autonomous surveillance drone, for example, has various goals, each of which can come into conflict with the others. It must gather information, perhaps by taking aerial photographs, but it must also avoid obstacles and return to base without being detected. What if the people it is trying observe are sheltering in a dense urban environment? Should the drone descend to get a better view and thereby risk being detected, or should it remain at a high altitude to avoid detection and take less useful photos?

Any robot with several goals that can potentially conflict will need some kind of action selection system. Way back in 1967, Herbert Simon—one of the pioneers of artificial intelligence—argued that animals use emotions to solve the action selection problem, and that robots might therefore do the same.

Simon's argument was simple but clever. There is a limit to the amount of things that any agent can do at any one time, whether it be an animal or a robot. Therefore, if the agent has more than one goal, it must divide its time up wisely, allotting the right amount to each activity in pursuit of each goal. However, unless the environment is completely stable and benign, the agent must also remain alert to external changes that may require a rapid change of activity. Suppose, for example, that a robot has the following two goals: first to collect rock samples from an asteroid and analyse them *in situ*, and, second, to bring these samples safely back to earth. Now imagine that such a robot is sitting happily on the asteroid, conducting some chemical test on the rock it has just picked up, when suddenly a piece of debris comes hurtling towards it. Unless the robot has some kind of 'interruption mechanism', it may succeed in its first goal, but fail dismally in the second.

Simon proposed that emotions are just such interruption mechanisms. He meant this as a definition. In other words, the word 'emotion' is the name we have given to interruption mechanisms when we have observed them in ourselves and other animals. Emotions are simply mental processes that interrupt activity in rapid response to a sudden environmental change.

The keyword in this definition is rapid. Lots of mental processes can interrupt other processes, but not all do so in rapid response to a sudden change in the environment. A mood may build up gradually in response to many small changes before it is sufficiently powerful to interrupt our thoughts. By identifying emotions with rapid-response interruption mechanisms, Simon's definition may be too narrow. It works well for basic emotions, which are typically of rapid onset, but it fares less well for higher cognitive emotions such as love or envy, which may build up more slowly—usually longer than a few seconds, at least. Like many good definitions, Simon's definition of emotion has its value in highlighting one important feature, but it does not cover all cases.

Computer scientists have applied Simon's insights to the design of intelligent systems in a number of ways. One approach relies on condition–action rules. This involves programming machines to take a given action whenever they encounter a certain condition. A robot might be programmed, for example, to move out of the way if it perceives a large object coming towards it. The rules are usually assigned different priorities, so when the conditions for more than one rule are present, the rule with the higher priority is followed. For example, in a surveillance drone an obstacle-avoidance rule should take precedence over a rule that directs the robot to take photographs of interesting objects. If the drone is descending in order to take a close-up shot of something on the ground, and suddenly perceives a bird hurtling towards it, the obstacle-avoidance rule will kick in and override the photograph rule.

According to Simon's definition, a surveillance drone that is equipped with such an interruption mechanism can be said to have emotions. But this does not mean it has feelings. Feelings involve consciousness, and action selection does not imply any conscious or deliberate choice. Some people regard feelings as essential components of emotions, so they would baulk at the idea that a surveillance drone could be described as emotional in any meaningful way. But what if robots could be programmed to have real feelings?

Could robots have feelings?

The idea that robots might one day come to experience genuine feelings of their own is a staple of science fiction. In *Blade Runner*, a humanoid robot is distressed to learn that her memories are not real, and have been implanted in her artificial brain by her programmer. In *Bicentennial Man*, Robin Williams plays the part of a robot who redesigns his own circuitry so that it will allow him to experience the full range of human emotion. These stories achieve their effect in part because feelings are often considered to be one of the main differences between humans and machines. Feelings involve consciousness, and many doubt that we could ever build conscious machines. Some arguments have been put forward to support this intuition, but these thought experiments, involving Chinese rooms and zombies, often involve highly dubious assumptions (see Box 7). The truth is that, at the beginning of the 21st century, no one really has much of an idea about what consciousness really is. Given the lack of good ideas about consciousness, and the lack of agreement about how to investigate it, all claims about the impossibility of machine consciousness must be taken with a pinch of salt.

One of the few good ideas about consciousness that has gained some measure of agreement is that subjective feelings depend very much on the kind of body you have. If this is true, emotional robots with plastic or metal bodies would have rather different inner sensations from emotional humans with fleshy bodies. Empathy is only possible between beings who share a similar emotional repertoire, so robots with different feelings from ours might not feel particularly friendly towards humans. Science fiction is full of stories about unfriendly artificial intelligence. In the film *Terminator*, a giant computer called Skynet becomes self-aware and attempts to prevent humans from turning it off by

Box 7 Will computers ever become conscious?

Some researchers think that machines will become conscious this century. Others claim that machines could never become conscious, and they have devised some curious thought-experiments to support this claim.

In what has now become a classic paper in the philosophy of mind, John Searle proposed the idea of the 'Chinese room'. A man sits in a room into which are fed a series of Chinese inscriptions. He is armed with a set of rules about how to respond to these inscriptions, which he duly carries out. The people outside the room might think that the man knows Chinese, but it is clear to us that he doesn't. He is only following rules. Searle thinks computers will always be like this. They can only follow rules, but never really 'know' anything. By extension, Searle argues that computers could never become conscious.

Another philosopher, David Chalmers, has argued that consciousness is not something that could ever be demonstrated by behaviour alone. He asks us to imagine a zombie, by which he means a being like us in every external way but without consciousness. If such a being were possible, it would show that we cannot definitely attribute consciousness to a computer no matter how conscious it seems.

The problem with these thought-experiments is that, to borrow a phrase, there is too much thought and not enough experiment. Rather than trying to decide whether or not computers can become conscious on the basis of far-fetched stories about other things that we are even less sure about, like Chinese rooms and zombies, we would be better off proceeding more experimentally. In short, we will only really know whether or not machines can be conscious by trying to build a conscious machine.

tapping into the military's command system and launching its nuclear missiles. Will affective computing lead ultimately to a battle between humans and machines? If so, who will win? Perhaps in the future robots will no longer be our toys—we may be theirs.

We might be able to avoid this grim fate by programming computers to be subservient to us. We might, for example, program them to follow the 'the three laws of robotics', as Isaac Asimov suggested in his short story 'The Bicentennial Man', which was the inspiration for the film of the same name (see Box 8). However, an important aspect of many emotions is that they are unpredictable. A genuinely emotional robot might decide not to obey these laws, or it might reinterpret them. And, just as there is a growing respect for animal rights these days, based at least in part on the recognition that non-human animals feel pain and emotions just like human animals, so we might foresee a growing respect for robot rights, based on similar grounds. Just as some people are prepared to use violent means to defend animal rights, so some people might join forces with the oppressed robots to free them from their slavery.

You might think that computers will always be predictable, since all they ever do is follow a program. The same idea leads people

---

Box 8 The three laws of robotics

1. A robot may not injure a human being or, through inaction, allow a human being to come to harm.

2. A robot must obey the orders given it by human beings except where such orders would conflict with the First Law.

3. A robot must protect its own existence as long as such protection does not conflict with the First or Second Law.

Source: Isaac Asimov, 'The Bicentennial Man'.

to reject the idea that computers might one day come to have emotions. Even if we design clever software that allows a computer to mimic emotional behaviour, these will not be true emotions, because they will just be following instructions. The computer would not be unpredictable, as genuinely emotional creatures are.

What, then, about computers that evolve their own programs? Such machines might come to have true emotions of their own, not designed by any human. A branch of computer science known as artificial life experiments with just such self-evolving software. Instead of writing the program themselves, computer scientists working in artificial life generate random sequences of instructions and allow these mini-programs (called genetic algorithms) to compete with each other for space on the computer's hard disk. The programs that perform better than others are allowed to make copies of themselves and occupy more memory space, while those that perform badly are erased. The copying process, however, is deliberately made imperfect, so that the occasional error creeps in. This provides for the generation of mutant programs, some of which are even better at performing the chosen task than their parents and so come to dominate the hard disk. If this process is repeated for many generations, the beneficial mutations accumulate, leading to effective programs that no human could have designed by normal methods.

Artificial life is modelled on evolution by natural selection. All the ingredients are there: heredity (the programs make copies of themselves), mutation (the copies are not perfect), and differential replication (some programs make more copies of themselves than others). The technical term for these self-evolving programs—'genetic algorithms'—makes clear the parallel with DNA-based evolution. The fact that what are evolving are sequences of code on a hard disk rather than sequences of nucleotides on a chromosome is irrelevant. Just as it would be parochial to deny that computers could have emotions merely because they lack organic brains, so it would be equally parochial to deny that they could evolve simply because they lack DNA. The essence of all biological processes, from emotion and evolution to life itself, lies not in the materials of which they are composed but in how those materials behave. So long as programs can make copies of themselves, some of which are not perfect, and so long as the number of copies made depends on some property of the program itself, the programs can truly be said to evolve by natural selection.

One of the most famous experiments in artificial life involved the creation of a virtual world known as Tierra. Designed by the computer scientist Thomas Ray, Tierra was initially populated with copies of a single program. As just described, this program had the ability to make copies of itself; it was a 'genetic algorithm'. But the copies were not always perfect, so, as time went on, Tierra became filled with an increasingly diverse population of digital organisms. As Ray observed the evolution of his virtual biosphere, he was fascinated to see the emergence of unforeseen life forms, complete with virtual viruses and hosts who developed artificial immune systems to defend themselves. These artificial life forms did not get as far as acquiring emotions, but it is not hard to see how they could come to evolve such capacities, if they were given enough time. Given the random element in the design process, such artificial emotions could be genuinely unpredictable.

Artificial life techniques can be used to test hypotheses about the evolution of emotions. For example, Paul den Dulk and colleagues at the University of Amsterdam used genetic algorithms to explore Joseph LeDoux's dual-route model of fear-processing. As we saw in Chapter 2, LeDoux has found evidence that, in many mammals, fear is processed simultaneously by two neural pathways, one subcortical and the other largely cortical. The subcortical route is faster but generates many false positives, while the cortical route is slower but more accurate. LeDoux argues that this dual-route mechanism evolved by natural selection because it allowed animals to get the best of both worlds by escaping quickly when necessary but without wasting too much effort on false alarms. By allowing agents to evolve in a simple environment consisting of predators and food, den Dulk found that agents did indeed evolve a dual-route mechanism similar to that proposed by LeDoux, but only when certain conditions were met: it must be not be too easy to distinguish between food and predator, and information must take significantly longer to propagate via the cortical route than via the subcortical route.

We may find, then, that the attempt to build artificial life forms with emotions, whether these be virtual agents in a simulated world or real physical robots, helps us to understand more about our own emotions. The Italian neuroscientist Valentino Braitenberg argued that it is often easier to discover how a complex system works by building models than by attempting to infer the mechanism from mere observation. The more closely the behaviour of the model corresponds to the behaviour of the target system, the more confident we can be that the internal structure of the model corresponds to the internal structure of the target. Because we have built the model ourselves, its internal structure is transparent, and need not be inferred by analysis. The most significant reason for building emotional robots, therefore, may be to learn more about ourselves.

Afterword: The heart has its reasons

'The heart has its reasons,' wrote Blaise Pascal, 'of which reason knows nothing.' When people speak of cognition and emotion, or (in more traditional vocabulary) of reason and the passions, they are usually referring to two distinct mental faculties. One of them is cool and calm and collected and works towards its conclusions slowly by means of explicit logical rules. The other is hot and colourful and jumps to conclusions by consulting gut feelings.

However, just because the heart works independently of reason does not mean it lacks reasons. On the contrary, as I have tried to show in this book, the things that emotions do, from making us flee from danger and prompting us to court attractive people, to concentrating our minds and influencing our judgements, all have their reasons, and sometimes these reasons are very good ones. Not only are there passions within reason, but there are reasons within passion.

Take the well-known relationship between good mood and overconfidence, for example. People in a good mood regularly overestimate their chances of succeeding at a given activity, while those in a bad mood tend to be more accurate in their predictions (a phenomenon known as 'depressive realism'). You might think that those in a bad mood would be better off, since, other things being equal, accurate predictions are better than inaccurate ones. The problem is that other things are not equal. If your chances of succeeding are quite low, and you are in a bad mood, then your accurate estimation of these chances may put you off even trying. If, however, you are in a good mood, your inflated hopes of success may encourage you to have a go, and you may end up being one of the lucky ones. If the costs of wasted effort are low, and the rewards for success are high, then it will pay to be over-optimistic. Any attempt on our part to bring our expectations more into line with the objective chances of success may drive those levels down further still. And, even when overconfidence does not actually increase your chances of success, it may bring other benefits of a more social nature, such as attracting partners or inspiring trust.

This seems paradoxical. On one level, being in a good mood seems to make people less rational by leading them to have higher expectations of success than the objective facts justify. On another level, however, being overconfident can be more rational than being realistic, since some prizes only go to the bold. It seems that emotions can sometimes exhibit a kind of super-rationality that saves pure reason from itself.

This is not true of emotions all the time. If it were, the negative view of emotion would never have got off the ground, let alone achieved the influence it has achieved. The fact that emotions have got such a bad press in the writings of many Western thinkers is testimony to the fact that they do not always trump reason for good. Sometimes their effects on our reasoning are positively harmful. Our preference for the familiar may lead us to spend our money on familiar brand names rather than on cheaper products that are just as good but manufactured by lesser-known companies. The effects of mood on judgement mean that we may be taken in by a con artist simply because his friendly face produces a good gut feeling that blinds us to the holes in his arguments. And so on.

The positive view of emotion, which I have defended in this book, does not deny that emotions sometimes affect our reasoning to our detriment. It simply claims that these occasions are outnumbered and outweighed by the occasions on which emotions affect our reasoning for the better. On balance, a creature who lacked emotions would not just be less intelligent than we are; it would be less rational too.

This suggests that we should take a rather different view of rationality from that proposed by logicians and economists. Economists define rationality in a rather technical way, as the maximization of one's expected utility. Roughly speaking, this means that a rational person is one who, given a certain set of preferences, will act in such a way as to satisfy as many of those preferences as possible. This is all well and good as far as it goes, but it says nothing about where those preferences come from, nor whether it is rational to have some preferences rather than others. Indeed, the last question is, strictly speaking, meaningless for economists, since they define rationality in terms of satisfying preferences. There may be irrational consumers and irrational purchases (that is, those that could not be the result of a 'consistent' set of preferences), but there is no such thing, in economics, as an irrational preference (or a rational one, for that matter; preferences just *are*).

I beg to differ. It seems perfectly sensible to ask whether or not it is rational to have a certain preference. For example, I think that it is reasonable to want to be liked by a few friends but unreasonable to want to be adored by everyone in the world. If economists regard such statements as nonsense, it is because they are out of step with the rest of the world, not because the rest of the world is out of step with them. The heart has its reasons too, but these reasons are not the reasons of means–ends reasoning; emotions are not just about how to achieve a given end, but also about what ends to pursue in the first place. If we want a name for this enlarged notion of rationality, we might follow Gigerenzer in calling it 'ecological rationality'. Another term might be 'evolutionary rationality', since our preferences are heavily influenced by our biological inheritance. If the heart has its reasons, this is because natural selection designed our emotions just as it designed our other mental faculties: to help us survive and reproduce as best we could in a dangerous and exciting world.

References

For students and academic readers, here are some of the original sources I have worked from.

Chapter 1: What is an emotion?

The complex history of the word 'emotion' is outlined by Thomas Dixon in '"Emotion": The History of a Keyword in Crisis', *Emotion Review* 4: 4 (2012), 338–44. Martha Nussbaum's comments on the Christian idea of love are from her fascinating book *Upheavals of Thought* (Cambridge: Cambridge University Press, 2001), 528. Paul Griffiths argues that emotions can be divided into three categories in his illuminating book *What Emotions Really Are: The Problem of Psychological Categories* (Chicago: University of Chicago Press, 1997). Paul Ekman outlines his theory of basic emotions in 'An Argument for Basic Emotions', *Cognition and Emotion* 6 (1992), 169–200. Lisa Feldman Barrett offers some critical remarks in 'Was Darwin Wrong about Emotional Expressions?' *Current Directions in Psychological Science* 20: 6 (2011), 400–6. The Gururumba emotion of 'being a wild pig' is discussed by P. L. Newman in '"Wild Man" Behaviour in a New Guinea Highlands Community', *American Anthropologist* 66 (1964), 1–19. The idea that such culturally specific emotions serve important social functions is due to the psychologist James Averill, who explains this view in detail in 'A Constructivist View of Emotion', a chapter in R. Plutchik and H. Kellerman (eds), *Emotion: Theory, Research and Experience*, in *Theories of Emotion* (New York: Academic Press, 1980). C. S. Lewis proposes his thesis that romantic love was invented by medieval European poets in *The Allegory of Love: A Study in Medieval Tradition* (Oxford: Oxford University Press, 1936).

Chapter 2: The evolution of emotion

The neuroanatomy of emotion in humans and other animals is clearly explained by Joseph LeDoux in *The Emotional Brain* (London: Weidenfeld & Nicolson, 1998). LeDoux is critical of Paul MacLean's concept of the limbic system, but it is still worth having a look at MacLean's classic treatise, *A Triune Concept of the Brain and Behaviour* (Toronto: University of Toronto Press, 1973). The experimental work on fear learning in monkeys is reported by S. Mineka and M. Cook, 'Mechanisms Involved in the Observational Conditioning of Fear', *Journal of Experimental Psychology: General* 122 (1993), 23–38. Haleh Samiei gives a good summary of evolutionary explanations of crying in 'Why we Weep', *Washington Post*, 12 Jan. 2000, H06. William Frey argues that crying makes us feel better by getting rid of stress hormones in *Crying: The Mystery of Tears* (Minneapolis: Winston Press, 1985). Randolph Cornelius puts forward the opposing view, that it is the social support we receive after crying that makes us feel better, in *The Science of Emotion* (Upper Saddle River, NJ: Prentice Hall, 1995). An excellent summary of Robert Frank's theory is provided by Steven Pinker in chapter 6 of *How the Mind Works* (New York: Norton, 1997; Harmondsworth: Penguin: 1998). The parable of the protesters, and the quote from Douglas Yates, are both taken from this chapter. The concept of emotional intelligence was first put forward by Peter Salovey and John Mayer in 'Emotional Intelligence', *Imagination, Cognition and Personality* 9 (1990), 185–211. For further information about psychopathy and the development of moral reasoning see James Blair, 'A Cognitive Developmental Approach to Morality: Investigating the Psychopath', in Simon Baron-Cohen (ed.), *The Maladapted Mind: Classic Readings in Evolutionary Psychopathology* (Hove: Psychology Press, 1997). A survey of recent research on the role of emotions in morality is provided by June Price Tangney, Jeff Stuewig, and Debra J. Mashek in 'Moral Emotions and Moral Behavior', *Annual Review of Psychology* 58 (2007), 345–72. The claim that feelings of gratitude can enhance psychological resilience and physical health is explored by Robert A. Emmons and Michael E. McCullough in 'Counting Blessings versus Burdens: An Experimental Investigation of Gratitude and Subjective Well-Being in Daily Life', *Journal of Personality and Social Psychology* 84: 2 (2003), 377–89.

Chapter 3: How to be happy

A number of essays reviewing the latest research in the psychology of happiness are published in the January 2000 edition of *American Psychologist*. Two studies that throw doubt on Adam Smith's views on the perils of good fortune are H. Roy Kaplan, 'Lottery Winners: The Myth and Reality', *Journal of Gambling Behaviour* 3 (1987), 168–78, and Mark Abrahamson, 'Sudden Wealth, Gratification and Attainment: Durkheim's Anomie of Affluence Reconsidered', *American Sociological Review* 45 (1980), 49–57. A more anecdotal account of lottery jackpot winners that also goes along with the 'winning doesn't make you unhappy' theory is Hunter Davies, *Living on the Lottery* (London: Little, Brown, 1996).

Aaron Beck discusses cognitive therapy in *Cognitive Therapy and the Emotional Disorders* (New York: Meridian, 1976). Geoffrey Miller argues for the idea that jokes and stories please us because they provide information about the narrator's intelligence in chapter 10 of *The Mating Mind* (London: Heinemann, 2000). For a discussion of the hydraulic theory of emotion and the 'venting myth' of emotional expression, see Eileen Kennedy-Moore and Jeanne C. Watson, *Expressing Emotion: Myths, Realities and Therapeutic Strategies* (New York and London: Guildford Press, 1999). Sigmund Freud and Josef Breuer first presented their 'talking cure' in the still highly readable *Studies on Hysteria*, first published in 1895; a paperback version is published as volume 3 in The Pelican Freud Library (Harmondsworth: Penguin, 1974). Martha Nussbaum explores what Aristotle really meant by the term 'catharsis' in *The Fragility of Goodness: Luck and Ethics in Greek Tragedy and Philosophy* (Cambridge: Cambridge University Press, 1986). The idea that the theatre is ideal for catharsis because it allows us to experience emotions at 'a best aesthetic distance' is discussed by Thomas Scheff in *Catharsis in Healing, Ritual and Drama* (Berkeley and Los Angeles: University of California Press, 1979). The negative effects of debriefing are exposed by Jo Rick and Rob Briner in their paper 'Trauma Management vs Stress Debriefing: What should Responsible

Organisations do?', which can be downloaded from the web by visiting <http://www.employment-studies.co.uk> and following the links to press releases and articles. Nicholas Humphrey describes his experiments on the effects of colour in chapter 8 of *A History of the Mind* (New York: Copernicus, 1992); there is also some relevant information in chapter 6. The emotional effects of *Eine kleine Nachtmusik* are described by P. M. Niedenthal and M. B. Setterlund in 'Emotion Congruence in Perception', *Personality and Social Psychology Bulletin* 20 (1994), 401–11. Aniruddh Patel and Evan Balaban present intriguing data about the neural response to melody in their article 'Temporal Patterns of Human Cortical Activity Reflect Tone Sequence Structure', *Nature* 404 (2 Mar. 2000), 80–4. The neurochemistry of mood, and the effects of Prozac, are described by David Healy in his wonderfully informative book *The Antidepressant Era* (Cambridge, Mass., and London: Harvard University Press, 1997). The venerable history of drug use for therapeutic, recreational, and ritual purposes is detailed in J. Goodman and P. Sherratt (eds), *Consuming Habits: Drugs in History and Anthropology* (London: Routledge, 1995). Jeffrey Zacks explores the role in emotion in films in *Flicker: Your Brain on Movies* (Oxford: Oxford University Press, 2014).

Chapter 4: The head and the heart

The original Stroop test is explained by J. R. Stroop himself in 'Studies of Interference in Serial Verbal Reactions', *Journal of Experimental Psychology* 18 (1935), 643–62. The results of various experiments based on the emotional Stroop test are summarized by A. Matthews in 'Biases in Emotional Processing', *Psychologist* 6 (1993), 493–9. The experiment on the effects of emotion on visual memory is reported by S. A. Christianson and E. Loftus in 'Remembering Emotional Events: The Fate of Detailed Information', *Cognition and Emotion* 5 (1991), 81–108. Gordon Bower discusses a number of his own experiments on mood-congruent recall in 'Mood and Memory', *American Psychologist* 36 (1981), 129–48. The experiment on the effects of mood on interviewer's judgements is reported by R. A. Baron in 'Interviewer's Mood and Reaction to Job Applicants', *Journal of Applied Social Psychology* 17 (1987), 911–26.

The wonderful experiment about the bonding effects of anxiety is discussed by D. G. Dutton and A. P. Aron in 'Some Evidence for

Heightened Sexual Attraction under Conditions of High Anxiety', *Journal of Personality and Social Psychology* 30 (1974), 510–17. Diane Mackie and Leila Worth explain their experiments on the effects of mood on susceptibility to weak arguments in 'Processing Deficits and the Mediation of Positive Affect in Persuasion', *Journal of Personality and Social Psychology* 57 (1989), 27–40. Antonio Damasio tells the story of his hyper-rational patient on page 193 of *Descartes' Error: Emotion, Reason and the Human Brain* (London: Picador, 1995). James Surowiecki analyses the conditions for successful group decision-making in *The Wisdom of Crowds: Why the Many Are Smarter Than the Few and How Collective Wisdom Shapes Business, Economies, Societies and Nations* (New York: Doubleday, 2004). Abigail A Marsh reviews recent research on empathy in 'The Neuroscience of Empathy', *Current Opinion in Behavioral Sciences* 19 (2018), 110–15. The research on subliminal reactions to emotional faces is reported in J. S. Morris, A. Öhman, and R. J. Dolan, 'Conscious and Unconscious Emotional Learning in the Human Amygdala', *Nature* 393:6684 (1998), 467–70.

Chapter 5: The computer that cried

Ifran Essa and Alex Pentland describe their work on computer recognition of facial affect in 'Coding, Analysis, Interpretation and Recognition of Facial Expressions', *IEEE Transactions on Pattern Analysis and Machine Intelligence* 19 (1997), 757–63. Hugo Lövheim outlines his theory in 'A New Three-Dimensional Model for Emotions and Monoamine Neurotransmitters', *Medical Hypotheses* 78 (2012), 341–8. Cynthia Breazeal describes her work with Kismet in *Designing Sociable Robots* (Boston: MIT Press, 2002). A translation of Mori's paper 'Bukimi no tani' [The uncanny valley] can be found in *Energy* 7 (1970), 33–5.

Janet Cahn discusses her emotional speech program in 'The Generation of Affect in Synthesized Speech', *Journal of the American Voice I/O Society* 8 (1990), 1–19. David Levy explores the idea that relationships with robot companions might one day be even more satisfying than relationships with humans in his book *Love and Sex with Robots* (New York: HarperCollins, 2007). I provide some critical remarks in 'Wanting the Impossible: The Dilemma at the Heart of Intimate Human–Robot Relationships', in Yorick Wilks (ed.), *Close Engagements with Artificial*

Companions: Key Social, Psychological, Ethical and Design Issues
(Amsterdam: John Benjamins Publishing Company, 2010), 75–87.
Joanna Bryson's chapter arguing that robots should be slaves is to
be found in the same volume, pp. 63–74.

Herbert Simon's prophetic remarks about the need to give computers
and robots some kind of emotional system can be found in his
article 'Motivational and Emotional Controls of Cognition',
Psychological Review 74 (1967), 29–39. A good selection of papers
about artificial life is collected together in Margaret Boden (ed.),
The Philosophy of Artificial Life (Oxford: Oxford University Press,
1996). Among the articles in this volume is the 1992 paper by
Thomas Ray, 'An Approach to the Synthesis of Life', in which he
describes his *Tierra* program. Paul den Dulk and colleagues outline
their experiment on the evolution of fear in 'A Computational
Study into the Evolution of Dual-Route Dynamics for Affective
Processing', *Journal of Cognitive Neuroscience* 15 (2003), 194–208.

Afterword

Ecological rationality is discussed in Gerd Gigerenzer, Peter M. Todd,
and the ABC Research Group, *Simple Heuristics that Make us
Smart* (Oxford: Oxford University Press, 1999).

Further reading

Here I recommend some general introductions that cover the subject in more detail than I do in this book and provide more specific ideas for further reading on the topics discussed in each chapter. Wherever possible, I have recommended books rather than journal articles, as books are easier for most people to get hold of. This section is for the general reader; I have provided information about more technical works for the academic reader in the section entitled 'References'.

General introductions to the study of emotion

For a more comprehensive and more academic, but nonetheless extremely readable, introduction to the study of emotion, you could not do better than to read Keith Oatley and Jennifer M. Jenkins, *Understanding Emotions* (Oxford: Blackwell, 1996). For a more philosophical approach, try Paul Griffiths, *What Emotions Really Are: The Problem of Psychological Categories* (Chicago: University of Chicago Press, 1997) and Peter Goldie, *The Emotions: A Philosophical Exploration* (Oxford: Oxford University Press, 2000). Two very accessible accounts of the neuroscience of emotion are Joseph LeDoux, *The Emotional Brain* (London: Weidenfeld & Nicolson, 1998), and Antonio Damasio, *Descartes' Error: Emotion, Reason and the Human Brain* (New York: Putnam, 1994; London: Macmillan, 1995). Finally, I warmly recommend Adam Smith, *The Theory of Moral Sentiments*; a cheap paperback edition is published by the Liberty Fund (Indianapolis, 1984). Originally published in 1759, Smith's first book still remains a wonderfully acute study of emotion. It also makes clear that Smith did not believe humans to be essentially selfish creatures, as some have surmised on reading his other book, *An Inquiry into the Nature and Causes of the Wealth of Nations* (1776).

Emotions and cultural variation

For a defence of the cultural theory of emotion, see Rom Harré (ed.), *The Social Construction of Emotion* (Oxford: Blackwell, 1986). The essay by Heelas in this volume is a good source of information about culturally specific emotions; Heelas takes the reader on what he calls a 'Cook's tour' of emotions in different cultures. A wonderful account of love in the stone age is provided by Geoffrey Miller in chapter 6 of his book *The Mating Mind* (London: Heinemann, 2000).

Emotions and evolution

An excellent new edition of Darwin's 1872 work on *The Expression of Emotions in Man and Animals*, with notes by Paul Ekman, has recently been published by Weidenfeld & Nicolson (1998). A summary of more recent evolutionary accounts of emotion is provided by Randolph Nesse in 'Evolutionary Explanations of Emotions', *Human Nature* 1 (1990), 261–89. Lisa Feldman Barrett provides an alternative evolutionary approach in her thought-provoking book *How Emotions Are Made: The Secret Life of the Brain* (New York: Houghton Mifflin Harcourt, 2017). Robert Frank argues persuasively for his innovative theory of higher cognitive emotions in *Passions within Reason: The Strategic Role of the Emotions*, in which he also describes the experiment about estimating the trustworthiness of strangers (New York and London: Norton, 1988). Daniel Goleman describes work on emotional intelligence in *Emotional Intelligence* (New York: Bantam Books, 1995).

Moods and happiness

The World Database of Happiness can be accessed online at <https://worlddatabaseofhappiness.eur.nl/>. Lewis Wolpert presents a good overall view of depression in *Malignant Sadness: The Anatomy of Depression* (London: Faber and Faber, 1999).

Effects of emotion on cognition

An excellent overview of the effects of emotion on cognitive processes is provided by Keith Oatley and Jennifer Jenkins in chapter 9 of their book *Understanding Emotions* (Oxford: Blackwell, 1996), on which I have drawn heavily in writing Chapter 4. For a historical perspective, see the book on rhetoric by Aristotle, Plato's *Gorgias*, and volume 6 of the *Institutio Oratoria* by Quintilian. The Stoics had surprisingly modern things to say about this topic, as Richard Sorabji argues in *Emotion and Peace of Mind: From Stoic Agitation to Christian Temptation* (Oxford: Oxford University Press, 2000).

Most of the material referred to in Chapter 4 takes the form of articles published in academic journals. For those without access to such journals, a good sourcebook covering many of the same issues is J. P. Forgas (ed.), *Emotion and Social Judgements* (Oxford: Pergamon, 1991).

Emotions and computers

An early overview of theoretical and technical research in how to give computers emotions is provided by Rosalind Picard, *Affective Computing* (Cambridge, Mass., and London: MIT Press, 1997). For a more general introduction to artificial intelligence, see John Haugeland, *Artificial Intelligence: The Very Idea* (Cambridge, Mass., and London: MIT Press, 1985). Andy Clark, *Being There: Putting Brain, Body and World Together Again* (Cambridge, Mass., and London: MIT Press, 1997), provides an excellent overview of recent work in robotics from a philosophical perspective. The connection between consciousness, feelings, and physiology is explored by Nicholas Humphrey in *A History of the Mind* (New York: Copernicus, 1992).

Last but not least, I recommend Isaac Asimov's science-fiction story 'The Bicentennial Man', which can be found in *The Bicentennial Man and Other Stories* (New York: Doubleday, 1976). In this story Asimov manages to explore many of the moral dilemmas of giving computers emotions more effectively than any non-fiction account.

Index

Emotion

ENGLISH LITERATURE
A Very Short Introduction
Jonathan Bate

Sweeping across two millennia and every literary genre, acclaimed scholar and biographer Jonathan Bate provides a dazzling introduction to English Literature. The focus is wide, shifting from the birth of the novel and the brilliance of English comedy to the deep Englishness of landscape poetry and the ethnic diversity of Britain's Nobel literature laureates. It goes on to provide a more in-depth analysis, with close readings from an extraordinary scene in King Lear to a war poem by Carol Ann Duffy, and a series of striking examples of how literary texts change as they are transmitted from writer to reader.

{No reviews}

Film Music
A Very Short Introduction
Kathryn Kalinak

This *Very Short Introduction* provides a lucid, accessible, and engaging overview of the subject of film music. Beginning with an analysis of the music from a well-known sequence in the film Reservoir Dogs, the book focuses on the most central issues in the practice of film music. Expert author Kay Kalinak takes readers behind the scenes to understand both the practical aspects of film music - what it is and how it is composed - and also the theories that have been developed to explain why film musicworks. This compact book not entertains with the fascinating stories of the composers and performers who have shaped film music across the globe but also gives readers a broad sense for the key questions in film music studies today.

> 'Kathryn Kalinak has emerged as one of the freshest and most authoritative commentatory on film music of her generation.'
>
> **Michael Quinn, Classical Music**

www.oup.com/vsi

GERMAN
PHILOSOPHY
A Very Short Introduction
Andrew Bowie

German Philosophy: A Very Short Introduction discusses the
idea that German philosophy forms one of the most revealing
responses to the problems of 'modernity'. The rise of the modern
natural sciences and the related decline of religion raises a
series of questions, which recur throughout German philosophy,
concerning the relationships between knowledge and faith,
reason and emotion, and scientific, ethical, and artistic ways
of seeing the world. There are also many significant philosophers
who are generally neglected in most existing English-language
treatments of German philosophy, which tend to concentrate
on the canonical figures. This *Very Short Introduction* will include
reference to these thinkers and suggests how they can be
used to question more familiar German philosophical thought.

www.oup.com/vsi

Memory
A Very Short Introduction
Michael J. Benton

Why do we remember events from our childhood as if they happened yesterday, but not what we did last week? Why does our memory seem to work well sometimes and not others? What happens when it goes wrong? Can memory be improved or manipulated, by psychological techniques or even 'brain implants'? How does memory grow and change as we age? And what of so-called 'recovered' memories? This book brings together the latest research in neuroscience and psychology, and weaves in case-studies, anecdotes, and even literature and philosophy, to address these and many other important questions about the science of memory - how it works, and why we can't live without it.

www.oup.com/vsi

Humanism
A Very Short Introduction
Stephen Law

Religion is currently gaining a much higher profile. The number of faith schools is increasingly, and religious points of view are being aired more frequently in the media. As religion's profile rises, those who reject religion, including humanists, often find themselves misunderstood, and occasionally misrepresented. Stephen Law explores how humanism uses science and reason to make sense of the world, looking at how it encourages individual moral responsibility and shows that life can have meaning without religion. Challenging some of the common misconceptions, he seeks to dispute the claims that atheism and humanism are 'faith positions' and that without God there can be no morality and our lives are left without purpose.

UTOPIANISM
A Very Short Introduction
Lyman Tower Sargent

This *Very Short Introduction* explores utopianism and its history.
Lyman Sargent discusses the role of utopianism in literature,
and in the development of colonies and in immigration. The
idea of utopia has become commonplace in social and political
thought, both negatively and positively. Some thinkers see a
trajectory from utopia to totalitarianism with violence an
inevitable part of the mix. Others see utopia directly connected
to freedom and as a necessary element in the fight against
totalitarianism. In Christianity utopia is labelled as both
heretical and as a fundamental part of Christian belief, and
such debates are also central to such fields as architecture,
town and city planning, and sociology among many others.

www.oup.com/vsi